MW01122646

THE

MONEY
TRACKER

A QUICK AND EASY WAY TO
KEEP TABS ON YOUR SPENDING

JUDY LAWRENCE

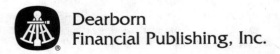

Dearborn
Financial Publishing, Inc.

This publication is designed to provide accurate and authoritative information in regard to the subject matter covered. It is sold with the understanding that the publisher is not engaged in rendering legal, accounting or other professional service. If legal advice or other expert assistance is required, the services of a competent professional person should be sought.

Managing Editor: Jack Kiburz
Interior Design: S. Laird Jenkins Corporation
Cover Design: Design Alliance, Inc.

ISBN 0-7931-1786-0

Dearborn books are available at special quantity discounts to use as premiums and sales promotions, or for use in corporate training programs. For more information, please call the Special Sales Manager at 800-621-9621, ext. 4384, or write to Dearborn Financial Publishing, Inc., 155 N. Wacker Drive, Chicago, IL 60606-1719.

CONTENTS

PREFACE

A Typical Day in Sara's Life

7:45 AM	*Stop for coffee, muffin and newspaper on the way to work.*
9:15 AM	*Chip in a few bucks at the office for Joe's birthday cake.*
10:00 AM	*Stop at the vending machine during break for pretzels and soda.*
12:00 noon	*Over lunch, stop for sandwich, pick up developed film and mail package. Buy a pair of inexpensive earrings from the street vendor on the way back to work.*
3:15 PM	*During break, grab bagel and coffee before sitting down with Angie to order some items from our favorite catalog.*
5:15 PM	*On the way home, pick up children from soccer practice, buy them a snack, then collect dry cleaning and new Scout uniform, refuel car, and buy Chinese takeout for dinner.*
8:00 PM	*Pledge $50 to local public television station.*

Finding the Money Trail

As a budget counselor, I see many clients who feel they have more than enough money to cover their bills and major expenses. And yet, while there may not be credit card or large loan repayments, these clients are often frustrated because they can't seem to get ahead. At the end of the month there never seems to be money left for saving, investing or special occasions. Like these clients, you may find yourself saying, "Where did all my money go?" on a regular basis. And, if you're like most people, you probably sat down with a note-pad and tallied all your regular expenses like loans, insurance premiums, credit card charges, utility bills, your children's music lessons, groceries, gas and lunches. Then, after arriving at that total and realizing that your income far exceeds these expenses, you exclaim once again, "Where *does* all my money go?"

If you have just repeated this routine for the umpteenth time, or if you recognize yourself in Sara's story, you have probably decided it is time to find out where your hard-earned cash is truly going. The Money Tracker will help you get your answer.

Using the Money Tracker

This convenient, portable Money Tracker provides a simple, organized format to help you immediately start tracking your daily, incidental spending. The Money Tracker will show you how you are spending those $40 ATM or debit withdrawals, which seem to slip away so quickly.

This handy Money Tracker will enable you to easily keep tabs on one of the most critical aspects of your personal finances: your out-of-pocket, day-to-day spending. Using the Money Tracker will provide a clear snapshot of your monthly spending as well as a year-end summary of expenses beyond the fixed usual bills. You can also create a more complete financial picture by incorporating the Money Tracker's summary of your daily spending into a monthly or annual budget book or software program.

Creating Your Budget

Even if you are already using a budgeting tool, the Money Tracker will boost its effectiveness, because the Money Tracker pinpoints both *planned* and *unplanned* spending that occurs throughout the course of your day. A good budgeting tool or spending plan focuses beyond daily expenditures to look at both your income and your anticipated expenditures over the course of the year—from fixed mortgages and VISA payments to Fido's rabies shots. An effective budget book also offers a way to plan for those occasional monthly and yearly expenses, like semiannual auto insurance, annual association dues or maintenance on your computer, that could otherwise sneak up and surprise you at the last minute.

And finally, an effective budget book provides you with a system for reining in all the financial information spinning around in your personal household orbit, including taxes, insurance, retirement, investments, bills, credit cards, ATM cards, and the newer cousins, debit cards and computer shopping. The best budgeting systems will guide you step-by-step through the process of compiling all this information. One that I'm partial to, perhaps because I wrote it, is *The Budget Kit,* which is available both in book and CD-ROM formats. *The Budget Kit* (and its previous version *COMMON CENT$*), which has sold more than 80,000 copies, takes a comprehensive approach to creating a personal and household budget that works.

The Psychology of Money

The Money Tracker not only shows you where your money goes but also can help reveal how you *feel* about money. Many people will half-jokingly say to me, "I really don't want to know where I spend my money." Some of them actually do realize where they fritter away money and aren't ready to change that habit just yet. Others, however, have psychological issues with money, and they might be afraid to take a closer look at their spending habits. Sometimes, they know subconsciously that they would be facing some realities that they would rather just ignore.

If you are like most people I have known and worked with in my budget counseling practice, financial problems are usually not *just* about spending more than you earn. More often, money problems are connected to an undercurrent of deeper emotional issues. These issues can range from relationship problems to a shame-based relationship with wealth to an obsessive-compulsive shopping behavior and much more. Whatever the case, it is important to realize that ongoing money problems often serve as a distraction and keep people from facing the real issues.

There are many excellent books on the market that address the emotional aspects of money and addictive spending in great detail. The Money Tracker is designed as an introductory guide to help you recognize any emotional obstacles you may have to changing your spending habits and attitudes. The journal pages provide a way to monitor your spending and emotional behavior on an ongoing basis.

Now, if you are ready to face the numbers, the Money Tracker stands ready to make it an easy and worthwhile experience. You will find tremendous rewards waiting for you when you take the time and make the effort to learn where your money is going.

21 DAYS TO
FINANCIAL SERENITY

"If you record it, you can change it."
—Marcia Sutton, PhD
author of *In Harmony, Resolving Stress*

21 Days Are Habit Forming

Many people have found that one way to change a habit successfully is to try a different behavior for 21 days. My book will introduce you to new money management habits and will show you how easy it is to make them part of your daily routine. The hardest part is the first step, but you've already taken that step by picking up this book.

In order to achieve freedom from financial *in*security, you can start by developing the habit of tracking your daily spending. People I meet often tell me that at first they found it difficult to get in the habit of keeping daily records. But then, as one client told me, "Near the end of the month, after about three weeks of keeping daily spending records, I noticed I was just doing it." So there you have it: 21 days to a new habit in action.

There are things you can do to ensure that once you get started you will keep going. For instance, those first weeks of tracking your expenses can often go easier if you have a strong incentive for making major changes in your life (a vacation, a new car, a new home, a new baby or freedom from debt). Keep reminding yourself of that new home or other great advantages you will gain and enjoy through adding this simple new habit to your life. *Also,* you can take steps to make your new habit easy to practice. For example, keep the Money Tracker and a sharp pencil close at hand so you can record expenses as they occur. Finally, you can keep yourself motivated through a daily or weekly system of rewarding yourself for adopting these new habits.

Dr. Sutton, in her book *In Harmony, Resolving Stress,* talks about modifying behavior by starting with self-recording. Once you start recording and monitoring an activity or behavior, you have information. From that information you can develop choices for making changes. In fact, clients have told me that once they started recording their expenses, they began spending less and saving more. You, too, will find that seeing the facts of how much you are really spending in each area of your life will move you out of denial into a conscious reality about money. From that vantage, you will be empowered to make more positive choices.

Success Stories

Over the years, clients and readers whose lives were in financial disarray have succeeded in turning their situations around. Many of their personal stories are in this book. They found the answer to the question, "Where does all my money go?" Utilizing that information helped them create effective, debt-free budget plans as they learned to live happily and successfully within their means. You will see a consistent theme in all of these stories: their newfound financial control leads to personal satisfaction, peace of mind and security in their lives. Ironically, by spending a little more time every day thinking about their finances, they spend a lot less time worrying about them.

The most dramatic story of new habits and persistence is by Glen Shane, who started out in debt, yet saved $100,000 in seven years! It all started with the simple action of recording and planning his spending every single day, so he had money left over to save and invest. You can read Glen's story in the January section of this book.

Spotting Patterns

After recording all your daily expenses for even a few weeks, you will notice a variety of personal spending patterns begin to emerge. Some people are amazed to see $30 a month going to books, yet many of the books stay on their bookshelves unread. Others immediately have their suspicions confirmed about the extent of their meals-out expense. Yet some aren't even aware of where they're eating a lot of those meals. Consider the case of one man who was shocked to realize he was spending $60 a month buying drinks and snacks from a vending machine. He decided to bring refreshments from home and to spend that $60 at a favorite restaurant with a companion.

The first thing to do is to *just notice* these patterns—don't criticize, blame or get upset, just notice. This is probably how you have been spending your money for a long time, but because it has been going on so long, it has become a reflex and doesn't seem excessive. As you notice these patterns, write them down for future reference and action.

Next, notice if there is a plan to your spending or if it is mostly impulsive. Here are some questions to ask yourself to determine the nature of your spending:

- Can you identify *priorities, needs* or *wants* in your spending?

- Do you notice that you tend to not pay attention to little financial details?
- Do you often say, "Well, it's really *only* x dollars"?
- In what one area do you seem to spend your money every day?
- Is there a consistent day or time to your spending, like payday or the first week paid, or lunch hour or weekends?
- When spending time with a friend, do you notice that you spend more?
- Do you buy individual bagels every day yet have a bag of them at home?
- Do you tend to forget beverages and lunch food at home and buy them at work instead?
- Do you make a list when you go to the store?
- Before buying something, how do you figure whether you can afford it?

Changing Your Patterns

Once you are aware of a situation, you can begin to think of creative ways to make changes. One couple had a hard time talking themselves out of buying things. In fact, they both knew they could easily talk each other *into* buying something. Even though they wanted to cut back on their spending and get out of debt, they would still tend to buy whatever they wanted. I suggested that when they shop together, they try alternating roles weekly or monthly as the "designated no-spender" person. That person serves as the naysayer to impulsive buys for that period, always keeping in mind the mutual goal of becoming debt-free. They liked the idea and worked with it.

Many couples use going out to dinner as their "time out of time" (as one client dubbed it), a way to escape the hectic family and work routine and spend time together. If dining out is an important part of your entertainment, can you find creative ways to dine out and still save money? One resourceful couple started going out for coffee and dessert. Another rediscovered the fun of picnics. Still others decided that dining out was important to them, while other areas of their spending were not. So, they painlessly cut back on those areas that added less value so they could afford to eat out. Each of them agreed this was not about depriving. Rather, by taking a look at how they spent their money, they could have more of what they really wanted *and* feel in control.

Many clients want to get into the habit of tucking money into a savings or investing plan on a regular basis. If you are like these clients, you might try simply saving all your pocket change plus one dollar every day and adding it to a monthly kitty. The key, of course, is to regularly deposit this money into some savings account or investment. It is not uncommon for this simple routine to result in saving and eventually investing from $50 to $100 a month.

You may actually decide, after reviewing your monthly spending records, that some of your patterns of spending are not too unrealistic, and this information can be reassuring. However, if your goal is to have more savings and investments for future wants, take a look at your spending to decide where you may want to cut back to achieve these goals.

Paying Attention to Your Emotions

Today's hectic lifestyles and obligations often force us to get so caught up in personal tasks and work routines that we forget to tune in to another side of ourselves—our emotions.

How do emotions affect spending money? Paying attention to emotions brings more balance to our lives by helping us develop healthier spending habits. The Money Tracker will guide you through this process.

Once you start to pay attention to your feelings, you might be surprised to discover how your basic attitudes and beliefs relate to spending patterns. Here are a few questions to help you uncover these connections:

- What are your moods when spending money?
- Do you experience joy, satisfaction or fulfillment with your purchases?
- Are you depressed before you go shopping? (This is often called "plastic therapy.")
- Do you ever feel compelled to buy something to please the salesperson?
- Do you buy only for others and not for yourself, and if so, do you know why?
- On payday, do you take care of all your bills first or treat yourself to things you want first?
- Do you hold off paying bills to make sure you have money for other expenses?

As you evaluate your responses, ask yourself whether or not your lifestyle and attitude are currently serving your best interest.

The Resource Guide at the end of the book lists several excellent books on the market that explore the psychology of money in detail. If you feel that your emotions are strong obstacles to changing destructive spending behaviors, you can start reading some of these books, consider getting professional help or look for a support group.

Most people find it revealing to reflect on where their attitudes come from. Often I will ask clients to tell me a little about how their family handled money and what messages they picked up from their childhood. Many times, I can almost see a light go on when clients make the "ah-ha" connection between a negative spending pattern or belief they have been practicing for many adult years and the childhood experience that originated it. That insight can go a long way towards freeing you from the old behavior and empowering you to make your own choices as an adult.

The Money Tracker will introduce you to the emotional side of money and help you to explore that aspect. If you feel resistant to this activity, you might want to give it a trial run before bypassing it altogether. Think about the highly successful couple who were spending beyond their income and never looked at credit card statements to see where the discretionary money was going. As I worked with them on their household budget, the couple one day announced they had made a connection between feelings and shopping and spending money. This was actually a very major first step towards moving out of their financial fog. For some people, just linking an action with a feeling is a powerful insight that can restore more control to their spending.

As you work through the Money Tracker, you'll find many tools to help you recognize and begin to come to terms with your feelings about money. There are questions to ask before spending, a splurge diary, suggestions for financial rewards and much more. Used in tandem with the Daily Money Tracker pages, the insights you gain will help you achieve financial serenity.

USING THE
MONEY TRACKER

Tracking Daily Expenses

The Money Tracker can be the first step towards creating a workable budget that complements your vision, your values and your goals. It will certainly provide you the insight you need for learning where your daily spending money is going. There are five Daily Money Tracker fill-in pages provided for each month (one for each week of the month). On these fill-in pages not only can you keep track of all your daily spending, but you also can record all ATM withdrawals or other ways you get cash (debit card, check, etc.). This way, you begin to see exactly how much cash you are actually spending each week and at the same time see where it is going.

Ideally, it will be handy to carry this book with you during the day in your purse, backpack, briefcase or car. If this doesn't fit your lifestyle, carry paper in your wallet or pocket to jot down daily spending information and then transfer these numbers to this book each day at your earliest convenience.

You also can incorporate this information into my budget book or software program, or the current product you are using, to develop a comprehensive budget that includes *all* the expenses for the month. Each week, if you take the totals from the categories and roll them into the budget, you can compare your actual expenses against anticipated expenditures.

The expense categories you see listed in the Daily Money Tracker sections were designed to help raise your awareness of the variety of ways that money can slip through your fingers on a daily basis. If you know that there are routine ways you spend money that are not listed on this Tracker, substitute those categories for any categories in which you never spend. For example, if you do not own pets but are an avid photographer, you could substitute film and equipment for pet food and grooming on the Tracker. Make whatever simple changes are needed to the categories in order to meet your needs. To that end, you might find it useful to review the Expense Supplement at the back of the book for a listing of additional types of expenses that can fall under the general categories listed on the Tracker. You also may want to add some of your own individual categories to the Expense Supplement, so you are consistent with how you track your expenses each month.

At first glance, you might think that certain categories hardly apply to you. If any expense category seems too incidental for you, go ahead and track the spending for a few weeks or months. Notice if any surprising information appears. One woman thought nothing of spending $20 for two bars of soap or $50 for oils and lotions until she started tracking it under toiletries. After seeing the total at the end of two months for toiletries alone, this expense took on a whole new perspective from just browsing and buying soaps and oils at will.

If you look at the list and are wondering where to record the phone bill, rent or car payment, you'll want to record those and similar once-a-month fixed expenses in your monthly budget book instead of in the Money Tracker. Remember, the role of the Money Tracker is to capture those daily, variable, out-of-pocket expenses. You will use the Tracker to keep tabs on items that are purchased by cash or check (though sometimes charged) and spent during your day-to-day routine. For instance, even though you may go to the utility company and pay your bill over lunch, that expense is usually a monthly expenditure and is recorded in your comprehensive budget book, software program or check register.

In some categories, such as medical expenses, there occur both fixed and variable costs. For some people, medical expenses are handled through insurance or paid monthly with the bills. They would find it most convenient to record those transactions in their monthly budget book. For others, there are numerous $5 or $10 out-of-pocket copayments during the month when taking the children to the doctor or picking up prescriptions. Those type of medical expenses are more variable and would get jotted down in the Money Tracker.

If you want to get a sense of how much you use your credit card for incidental expenses, you can use the Money Tracker to track your credit card charges. Using a highlighter or colored pen or circling those expenses you have charged could help you distinguish the expense as a charge and enable you to get a better sense of your credit habits.

The sample Daily Money Tracker at the end of this chapter can give you a better idea how this all works.

Yearly Summary

You will find the Daily Money Tracker *Yearly Summary* after the December section. Here is where you log your monthly totals for each category after adding up the weekly totals for each month. Once you have completed your first yearly summary, you will have a better picture of your monthly out-of-pocket spending. Even before then, as you compile the Summary, you will already begin to uncover spending patterns and see where the big spending areas are. You also can be quickly rewarded when you see the cumulative result of dramatic, calculated *decreased* spending in selected categories.

If you have also been regularly recording your weekly totals in your budget book, the yearly summary information from the Money Tracker also will be *reflected* in the yearly totals of your budget book.

Using the ATM and Debit Withdrawal Log

Used correctly, debit and ATM cards can provide valuable convenience today for busy people. On the other hand, these cards, along with the long-established wallet full of credit cards, can allow you to slip into more unconscious and unac-countable spending habits than ever before. The convenience of ready cash also has tended to speed up the rate of spending. As a result, unless you have a convenient method for reining in these transactions, you will find yourself facing financial chaos.

Think about your own cash retrieval habits: How do you get cash when you need it? Do you write a check? Or do you add $20 to your grocery bill? Or do you use your debit card and add cash to the purchase? Or perhaps, you withdraw cash with your ATM card or you get a cash advance with your credit card. It is important to think through how you obtain cash, because each way has a different cost associated with it.

As you probably know, the cash advance is the most ex-pensive way to get cash. Even if you pay your credit card bills in full each month, you will be charged a finance charge from the day of the transaction. If this is your usual method, on your next statement, find the finance charge for the cash advance section and see how much it costs you each month. The information is usually at the bottom of the page with all the other, often overlooked information. This cost varies from charge account to charge account but on average is closer to 18 percent. Once you pay attention to these costs and see how quickly they add up, you will be more motivated to find and use less expensive methods for getting cash.

On the bottom of the Daily Money Tracker form there is a space to record how much money you withdraw each day through your ATM or debit card. The ATM and Debit Withdrawal form is a separate record from the other expense categories. Those expense categories actually will reflect where much of the ATM and debit cash is going. If rather than using an ATM or debit card you customarily cash checks, or add a cash allotment to your purchase or raise cash in any other way, you will want to adapt the Money Tracker so that it adequately reflects your cash sources and amounts.

The purpose of tracking all these details is to help you become aware of all your money patterns. For instance, if you frequent ATM machines, notice whether you withdraw cash every day or once a week. Do you withdraw small or large amounts? Are you aware of the service fee associated with each ATM withdrawal? How many withdrawals can you have before the fees kick in? Are there less costly ways to obtain this cash?

After seeing your cash withdrawal spending pattern for a few months, you may be inspired to change it. Perhaps you will choose to withdraw larger amounts per trip and curb the number of visits. Doing so can be a big relief in terms of the frequent trips, time, inconvenience and cost, as well as the recordkeeping in the check register. Alternatively, you might choose to shop for a bank that provides free ATM transactions at all or selected terminals. Then again, you might find it cheaper and not too inconvenient to go to the bank teller.

In the meantime, you are keeping records of all these transactions in your checkbook register, aren't you? After seeing hundreds of household records, I know what many of those registers look like in the beginning—scanty to empty. Aside from helping you find out whether you need to change the frequency and nature of your cash retrieval habits, there is potentially an even greater benefit to tracking your ATM and debit withdrawals. By keeping an eye on these transactions, you can avoid the $20 to $200 in nonsufficient fund (NSF) charges that you previously may have had each month.

If you are like many people I meet, there may be a stack of unopened bank statements for the last six months sitting in your drawer somewhere. If it is any comfort to you, there are many people I have met whom I call "closet statement phobics." These are bright professionals who really have no clue how to balance or figure out their bank statements and are too embarrassed to admit this or get help. I helped one family save $200 in NSF charges every month by teaching them how to manage their bills and expenses and keep the checkbook balanced.

What To Do with All Those Slips of Paper

ATM slips usually can end up as crumpled pieces of paper unless you have a system. Keep an envelope in the back of this book for ATM and debit slips. As soon as you record the information here and in your check register, toss them—but not where someone can easily pick them up and read your account information!

I highly recommend recording all slips of paper—ATMs, receipts and charge slips—as soon as possible, preferably by day's end. Then toss all that paper (unless you need a receipt for returning an item, your taxes or other verification) and forget about it. Get the clutter out of your life and out of your mind. I worked with one woman who wanted to be sure to record all her spending in her budget book, so she saved every single receipt. When I saw the 12 gallon bags of receipts, one for each month, I recommended a new approach.

Aside from containing clutter, there is another valuable benefit to regularly recording your receipts. Writing information down in a timely fashion plays a very significant role in changing your spending habits. It is the hands-on action of writing it all down, totalling the numbers and comparing them with the previous numbers that causes a change in your consciousness and subsequently a transformation of your spending patterns.

Recognizing Your Feelings about Money

To help tune in to the emotional side of money, I have included some extra tools in the Money Tracker. At the beginning of each month I have listed a few questions. Consider this your "stop, look and listen" approach. Stop and notice what's going on in your head and in your gut before unconsciously spending. These questions may be enough to bring you back in touch with what you are feeling and doing during your spending. Keeping the daily records also will provide meaningful information.

The Monthly Money Journal following each set of Daily Money Trackers is your place for jotting down any insights or reflections about the previous month's overall spending.

If you want to explore a more serious side of your feelings and money, the Splurge Diary and the Victory Diary at the end of each month provide questions to guide you through a review of each splurge or victory event.

Alternatives to Spending Money

Review the list of suggestions on the Alternative Activities pages. These are no-cost or low-cost ideas for other things to do when you have a strong urge to spend money impulsively. Add many of your own creative ideas. Think of these pages as your resource for fun.

You may want to think of some budget-friendly ways to reward yourself when you make it through a spending urge with your money intact, when you saved money for the month in a particular category or made a specific desired change. Sometimes, you may get so caught up in your desire to change or improve that you forget to take time to congratulate and reward yourself for a job well done.

Lifetime Habit or Temporary Task?

Once you get in the habit of recording your daily spending, you may wonder how long you will keep doing this—keeping records, evaluating your spending and reviewing your attitude about spending. The choice is yours. Tracking your expenses may be a short-term experience to put you back on course or it may become—as it has for many—a long-established, comfortable habit that becomes a valued part of your life. These approaches vary from person to person.

Eventually, after a period of recordkeeping, many people develop a clear sense of their spending habits and establish their own financial guidelines and priorities along with a strong discipline. They don't always feel the need to actually continue keeping records until something changes. A new baby, a college-bound child, a new home, a job change or an ailing parent, each can be the event that activates a shift in financial goals and leads to a renewed tracking activity to establish a new budget.

On the other hand, the people whose success stories you will read at the beginning of each month have used *The Budget Kit* and decided to keep daily spending records indefinitely. They find that this routine brings them great financial rewards, security and peace of mind. The same may be true for you.

Like the people in the monthly success stories, no matter where or when you are starting, once you begin tracking your daily expenses, you too, can make wise money decisions and enjoy financial freedom. The goal is to help you become more tuned-in to your money and guide you to your own sense of financial control, self-confidence and money savvy.

SAMPLE WEEK OF: _5-11_ _*Charged items_

HOME	MON	TUES	WED
Groceries	14		
Meals Out	5	7	23
Snacks, Beverages, Liquor	6	1.50	6
Supplies, Furnishings	15.79		
TRANSPORTATION			
Gas, Public Transportation	16.70		
Vehicle Expense			
PERSONAL CARE			
Clothing, Accessories	40*		
Laundry, Shoe Care	15		
Hair Care, Toiletries		25	
Nails, Massage			
ENTERTAINMENT			
Movies, Videos			
CDs, Books			
Hobbies, Sports, Gym			
HEALTH CARE			
Prescriptions, Supplements	10	25	
Doctors, Dentists			
CHILDREN			
Child Care, Sitter	15		
Allowance, School Expense	79.53	Uniform	
PETS			
Food, Supplies, Grooming			10.73
MISCELLANEOUS			
Copies, Office Supplies		2.30	
Gifts, Cards			
~~Lottery~~ Film	9.78		
Tithe, Donations			
TOTAL	226.80	60.80	39.73
ATM WITHDRAWALS	80		40
DEBIT CASH WITHDRAWALS	60		

THUR	FRI	SAT	SUN	TOTAL
125				139
12	47.78*			94.78
	4.25			17.75
		73.80*	47.30	136.89
	10.59			27.29
	Car wash	9		9
		56.40*		96.40
				15
		13.25		38.25
17				17
	6	40		46
16.73				16.73
		17.63		17.63
				35
10				10
	10			25
20.25			20	119.78
		35 Vet		45.73
		9.70		12
		5		5
				9.78
200.98	78.62	259.78	67.30	934.01
80	20	70	40	330
50		50		160

JANUARY

Questions to ponder when reviewing
finances or right before spending . . .

**Is there one thing in particular I would like to change this
year about my spending or attitude towards money?**

Do I need to start putting aside money to pay off my taxes?

**How much would I have to save each month to have
enough money saved ahead this year for Christmas?**

---

*"When I started keeping records, it was like an awakening. In
the last seven years I have saved $100,000 thanks to your book."*

Before I kept track of my spending, I never had money. First of
all, I didn't like being in debt. I didn't like the creditors calling the
house and knocking at the door or getting notices in the mail. I
wanted to stop this way of living and get my spending and debt
under control. I was tired of not being able to get credit and always owing money. I wanted to sleep comfortably. And now I do.

I was 42 years old, making $31,000 and in debt. When I
started keeping records that year it was like an awakening. I

finally had an idea of what I was receiving, what I was spending and what I *wasn't* saving.

That first year, I had a lot more money left over than I did before I kept records. I could see how I could cut back in one area and increase in another area. I realized I could save money if I paid my bills on time. It took two years to clear up all my debt and to start putting money in my pockets instead of the creditor's.

My goals in the beginning were to be debt-free, start investing in savings for myself and have a retirement that would be comfortable, so I wouldn't have to worry about Social Security. When I was younger I didn't think about retirement, so when I started at age 42, I knew I would have to save a lot more. I knew I could do it, and I know others can, too. No one is going to do it for you, however. You have to be responsible for your own retirement.

Now I am very conscious of how I handle my money. If I don't spend it, I record what I didn't spend, and then I actually put that amount into savings. That's the big difference. I never really live beyond my means, but I am not depriving myself of anything. I have anything I want. When I watch how other people spend money, I can easily see how they could save $30 to $40 a week. Just brown-bagging my lunch saves me $5 to $6 a day. That's about $120 a month.

I'm elated. Your budget book made me aware of my spending habits and helped me keep everything in perspective. I love keeping these records daily. It is not a chore. Now it is just a part of me. The bills always get paid on time. My mortgage is paid off with the extra money going to savings. Each year I exceed my savings goal and now have savings of more than $100,000 and emergency money to take out if needed. That to me is a real sense of freedom.

Glen Shane, Bronx, N.Y.
Social Worker, $50,000/yr.
One Child, Age 14

JANUARY WEEK OF: _____

HOME	MON	TUES	WED
Groceries			
Meals Out			
Snacks, Beverages, Liquor			
Supplies, Furnishings			
TRANSPORTATION			
Gas, Public Transportation			
Vehicle Expense			
PERSONAL CARE			
Clothing, Accessories			
Laundry, Shoe Care			
Hair Care, Toiletries			
Nails, Massage			
ENTERTAINMENT			
Movies, Videos			
CDs, Books			
Hobbies, Sports, Gym			
HEALTH CARE			
Prescriptions, Supplements			
Doctors, Dentists			
CHILDREN			
Child Care, Sitter			
Allowance, School Expense			
PETS			
Food, Supplies, Grooming			
MISCELLANEOUS			
Copies, Office Supplies			
Gifts, Cards			
Lottery			
Tithe, Donations			
TOTAL			
ATM WITHDRAWALS			
DEBIT CASH WITHDRAWALS			

THUR	FRI	SAT	SUN	TOTAL

JANUARY WEEK OF: _____

HOME	MON	TUES	WED
Groceries			
Meals Out			
Snacks, Beverages, Liquor			
Supplies, Furnishings			
TRANSPORTATION			
Gas, Public Transportation			
Vehicle Expense			
PERSONAL CARE			
Clothing, Accessories			
Laundry, Shoe Care			
Hair Care, Toiletries			
Nails, Massage			
ENTERTAINMENT			
Movies, Videos			
CDs, Books			
Hobbies, Sports, Gym			
HEALTH CARE			
Prescriptions, Supplements			
Doctors, Dentists			
CHILDREN			
Child Care, Sitter			
Allowance, School Expense			
PETS			
Food, Supplies, Grooming			
MISCELLANEOUS			
Copies, Office Supplies			
Gifts, Cards			
Lottery			
Tithe, Donations			
TOTAL			
ATM WITHDRAWALS			
DEBIT CASH WITHDRAWALS			

THUR	FRI	SAT	SUN	TOTAL

JANUARY   WEEK OF: _____

HOME	MON	TUES	WED
Groceries			
Meals Out			
Snacks, Beverages, Liquor			
Supplies, Furnishings			
TRANSPORTATION			
Gas, Public Transportation			
Vehicle Expense			
PERSONAL CARE			
Clothing, Accessories			
Laundry, Shoe Care			
Hair Care, Toiletries			
Nails, Massage			
ENTERTAINMENT			
Movies, Videos			
CDs, Books			
Hobbies, Sports, Gym			
HEALTH CARE			
Prescriptions, Supplements			
Doctors, Dentists			
CHILDREN			
Child Care, Sitter			
Allowance, School Expense			
PETS			
Food, Supplies, Grooming			
MISCELLANEOUS			
Copies, Office Supplies			
Gifts, Cards			
Lottery			
Tithe, Donations			
TOTAL			
ATM WITHDRAWALS			
DEBIT CASH WITHDRAWALS			

THUR	FRI	SAT	SUN	TOTAL

JANUARY WEEK OF: _____

HOME	MON	TUES	WED
Groceries			
Meals Out			
Snacks, Beverages, Liquor			
Supplies, Furnishings			
TRANSPORTATION			
Gas, Public Transportation			
Vehicle Expense			
PERSONAL CARE			
Clothing, Accessories			
Laundry, Shoe Care			
Hair Care, Toiletries			
Nails, Massage			
ENTERTAINMENT			
Movies, Videos			
CDs, Books			
Hobbies, Sports, Gym			
HEALTH CARE			
Prescriptions, Supplements			
Doctors, Dentists			
CHILDREN			
Child Care, Sitter			
Allowance, School Expense			
PETS			
Food, Supplies, Grooming			
MISCELLANEOUS			
Copies, Office Supplies			
Gifts, Cards			
Lottery			
Tithe, Donations			
TOTAL			
ATM WITHDRAWALS			
DEBIT CASH WITHDRAWALS			

THUR	FRI	SAT	SUN	TOTAL

JANUARY WEEK OF: _____

HOME	MON	TUES	WED
Groceries			
Meals Out			
Snacks, Beverages, Liquor			
Supplies, Furnishings			
TRANSPORTATION			
Gas, Public Transportation			
Vehicle Expense			
PERSONAL CARE			
Clothing, Accessories			
Laundry, Shoe Care			
Hair Care, Toiletries			
Nails, Massage			
ENTERTAINMENT			
Movies, Videos			
CDs, Books			
Hobbies, Sports, Gym			
HEALTH CARE			
Prescriptions, Supplements			
Doctors, Dentists			
CHILDREN			
Child Care, Sitter			
Allowance, School Expense			
PETS			
Food, Supplies, Grooming			
MISCELLANEOUS			
Copies, Office Supplies			
Gifts, Cards			
Lottery			
Tithe, Donations			
TOTAL			
ATM WITHDRAWALS			
DEBIT CASH WITHDRAWALS			

THUR	FRI	SAT	SUN	TOTAL

MONTHLY MONEY JOURNAL

(Notes/Reflections/Insights/Progress)

Use these pages to jot down your thoughts and experiences with money as you go through the month.

Did you notice any spending patterns?

....

....

....

Are there consistent thoughts or feelings you noticed when spending at certain times or on specific items?

....

....

....

Were you surprised at how much you spent in certain areas?

....

....

....

Were you delighted to see how long your money lasted or how little you spent in some areas?

....

....

....

Have you come up with changes you want to make?

....

....

....

Other comments:

....

....

....

....

SPLURGE DIARY

Use these pages for those times when your spending is totally unplanned and way over budget. By recording your feelings and circumstances about a particular spending event you can begin to get in touch with some deeper reasons for spending.

Date	What I bought or spent money on	Amount	Cash	Charge
....	....	....	....	....
....	....	....	....	....
....	....	....	....	....
....	....	....	....	....

What happened right before the spending?

....

....

....

How was I feeling at that time?

....

....

....

How did I feel during the spending?

....

....

....

How did I feel a few hours later?

....

....

....

Sample feelings: *depressed, angry, excited, empty, lonely, guilty, shamed, remorseful, anxious, frantic, bored, nervous, powerful, deserving, noticed, confused, worried, fearful, hopeless, accepted, resentful, overwhelmed, tired, needy, disappointed*

How did I feel the next day and/or a week later?

....

....

....

What did I do as a result of that spending?

....

....

....

What did I learn about myself (my habits, feelings, patterns, thoughts)?

....

....

....

What unmet needs am I possibly trying to meet through my spending?

....

....

....

Who or what do these feelings remind me of from my past?

....

....

....

Next time, what can I do to replace the spending urge?
(See Alternative Activities List.)

....

....

....

Changes I've made since that spending:

....

....

....

Notes/Reflections/Insights:

VICTORY DIARY

Use these pages for those times when you *successfully did not give in* to your spending urges. Changing your spending patterns is a very positive and significant event, so acknowledge yourself on these occasions.

Date	What I *almost* bought or spent money on	Amount	Cash	Charge
....	....	....	....	....
....	....	....	....	....
....	....	....	....	....
....	....	....	....	....

What happened right before the spending urge?

....

....

....

How was I feeling at that time?

....

....

....

What did I do to *replace* the spending urge?

....

....

....

How did I feel immediately after deciding *not* to spend the money?

....

....

....

Sample feelings: *powerful, in charge, victorious, calm, relaxed, happy, proud, content, honest, satisfied, hopeful, validated, accepted, delighted, responsible, free*

How did I feel a few hours later?

....

....

....

How did I feel the next day and/or a week later?

....

....

....

What did I learn about myself (my habits, feelings, patterns, beliefs)?

....

....

....

I am proud of myself because:

....

....

....

How did I reward myself (praised myself, read a book, prepared a pleasant meal, took a nap, spent time on crafts or hobbies, took a drive, walked the dog, etc.)?

....

....

....

Notes/Reflections/Insights:

ALTERNATIVE ACTIVITIES LIST

For Replacing Spending Urges

Having the urge to spend, for some people, can be a very powerful feeling, so it is not easy to just *will it away*. When the urge comes up, you might try postponing it by engaging in another activity. I have listed some low-cost, no-cost activity ideas to help you gradually find ways to replace those urges with new, more positive behavior.

Try them out and see what works best for you. Your ideas are probably the most creative, so be sure to add many of your own.

These suggestions are especially effective if you are at the stage where you recognize you have behaviors and feelings associated with spending money. If your spending behavior has become much more serious and feels out of control, please see the Resource Guide in the back of the book for help.

Instead of spending at this particular time, I can . . .

✔ *Use the 24-hour technique: Tell yourself that you can buy this item. You can buy it tomorrow. You are choosing to wait 24 hours.*

- ✔ *Call a supportive friend or sponsor and talk about the events of the day and your feelings*

- ✔ *Take a walk or a drive, bike ride, hike, rollerblade or go to the gym*

- ✔ *Read a good story in a book or magazine*

- ✔ *Spend time on your favorite hobby or craft*

- ✔ *Watch a great movie*

- ✔ *Take in a museum, zoo or the botanical gardens*

- ✔ *Play with your children or your pets*

- ✔ *Have your partner give you a massage*

- ✔ *Take a bath or a nap*

- ✔ *Listen to music*

- ✔ *Meditate*

- ✔ *Now add your own*

My favorite activities to do or new things to try are:

....

....

....

....

....

FEBRUARY

Questions to ponder when reviewing
finances or right before spending . . .

**How can I pay more than the minimum payment on
my credit card bills from last year, so I can save
hundreds of dollars of extra interest payments?**

Am I satisfied with the way I am spending my money?

Do I fully enjoy the things I already have?

---

*"I no longer have to be a victim to my whims and
fancies. Recording expenses has helped me learn how I can
have the power to be effective with my money."*

I was raised in a family where financial planning was not
well executed. My mother did not have a lot of training in
budgeting and planning because she had been raised in
wealth. She charged a lot of things. Even as a child, I knew
that was not good, but I didn't know anything about the budgeting process.

About 14 years ago, I started using a budget book and
learned how to handle money. I disciplined myself to record

my spending every day and started seeing where my money was going and where I was spending too much. This information gave me hope. I slowly began to realize I had the power to control my own spending. With continual budget practice and consistent recordkeeping, I began to feel inspired by my ability to handle money. I finally believed I could become really good with money as I gained competence in the area of finances. These methods gave me the gestalt with which to work.

I used to experience money as a whim—it came in, it went out. I have learned I don't have to be a victim to whims and fancies anymore. If I make mistakes, I can pick myself up and move right on again. The success I've had with keeping records and planning my expenses has given me a boost to go ahead and start thinking of long-range financial goals. My husband and I have been very successful with that planning. We have educated two successful children and have traveled extensively.

By learning how to manage money, I have secured a TSA (a retirement plan) at work and am interested in many financial areas—areas I wouldn't have been interested in before. This practical experience has helped me see I was capable of gaining control and of becoming an astute money manager.

I'm planning to retire soon and start a private practice in educational therapy. And, it all began with learning how to keep records of my daily spending.

Sara Phillips Combs, Lafayette, Calif.
Special Education Resource Specialist, Age 60
Two Children, Two Grandchildren

FEBRUARY WEEK OF: _____

HOME	MON	TUES	WED
Groceries			
Meals Out			
Snacks, Beverages, Liquor			
Supplies, Furnishings			
TRANSPORTATION			
Gas, Public Transportation			
Vehicle Expense			
PERSONAL CARE			
Clothing, Accessories			
Laundry, Shoe Care			
Hair Care, Toiletries			
Nails, Massage			
ENTERTAINMENT			
Movies, Videos			
CDs, Books			
Hobbies, Sports, Gym			
HEALTH CARE			
Prescriptions, Supplements			
Doctors, Dentists			
CHILDREN			
Child Care, Sitter			
Allowance, School Expense			
PETS			
Food, Supplies, Grooming			
MISCELLANEOUS			
Copies, Office Supplies			
Gifts, Cards			
Lottery			
Tithe, Donations			
TOTAL			
ATM WITHDRAWALS			
DEBIT CASH WITHDRAWALS			

THUR	FRI	SAT	SUN	TOTAL

FEBRUARY   WEEK OF: _____

HOME	MON	TUES	WED
Groceries			
Meals Out			
Snacks, Beverages, Liquor			
Supplies, Furnishings			
TRANSPORTATION			
Gas, Public Transportation			
Vehicle Expense			
PERSONAL CARE			
Clothing, Accessories			
Laundry, Shoe Care			
Hair Care, Toiletries			
Nails, Massage			
ENTERTAINMENT			
Movies, Videos			
CDs, Books			
Hobbies, Sports, Gym			
HEALTH CARE			
Prescriptions, Supplements			
Doctors, Dentists			
CHILDREN			
Child Care, Sitter			
Allowance, School Expense			
PETS			
Food, Supplies, Grooming			
MISCELLANEOUS			
Copies, Office Supplies			
Gifts, Cards			
Lottery			
Tithe, Donations			
TOTAL			
ATM WITHDRAWALS			
DEBIT CASH WITHDRAWALS			

THUR	FRI	SAT	SUN	TOTAL

FEBRUARY   WEEK OF: _____

HOME	MON	TUES	WED
Groceries			
Meals Out			
Snacks, Beverages, Liquor			
Supplies, Furnishings			
TRANSPORTATION			
Gas, Public Transportation			
Vehicle Expense			
PERSONAL CARE			
Clothing, Accessories			
Laundry, Shoe Care			
Hair Care, Toiletries			
Nails, Massage			
ENTERTAINMENT			
Movies, Videos			
CDs, Books			
Hobbies, Sports, Gym			
HEALTH CARE			
Prescriptions, Supplements			
Doctors, Dentists			
CHILDREN			
Child Care, Sitter			
Allowance, School Expense			
PETS			
Food, Supplies, Grooming			
MISCELLANEOUS			
Copies, Office Supplies			
Gifts, Cards			
Lottery			
Tithe, Donations			
TOTAL			
ATM WITHDRAWALS			
DEBIT CASH WITHDRAWALS			

THUR	FRI	SAT	SUN	TOTAL

FEBRUARY WEEK OF: _____

HOME	MON	TUES	WED
Groceries			
Meals Out			
Snacks, Beverages, Liquor			
Supplies, Furnishings			
TRANSPORTATION			
Gas, Public Transportation			
Vehicle Expense			
PERSONAL CARE			
Clothing, Accessories			
Laundry, Shoe Care			
Hair Care, Toiletries			
Nails, Massage			
ENTERTAINMENT			
Movies, Videos			
CDs, Books			
Hobbies, Sports, Gym			
HEALTH CARE			
Prescriptions, Supplements			
Doctors, Dentists			
CHILDREN			
Child Care, Sitter			
Allowance, School Expense			
PETS			
Food, Supplies, Grooming			
MISCELLANEOUS			
Copies, Office Supplies			
Gifts, Cards			
Lottery			
Tithe, Donations			
TOTAL			
ATM WITHDRAWALS			
DEBIT CASH WITHDRAWALS			

THUR	FRI	SAT	SUN	TOTAL

FEBRUARY WEEK OF: _____

HOME	MON	TUES	WED
Groceries			
Meals Out			
Snacks, Beverages, Liquor			
Supplies, Furnishings			
TRANSPORTATION			
Gas, Public Transportation			
Vehicle Expense			
PERSONAL CARE			
Clothing, Accessories			
Laundry, Shoe Care			
Hair Care, Toiletries			
Nails, Massage			
ENTERTAINMENT			
Movies, Videos			
CDs, Books			
Hobbies, Sports, Gym			
HEALTH CARE			
Prescriptions, Supplements			
Doctors, Dentists			
CHILDREN			
Child Care, Sitter			
Allowance, School Expense			
PETS			
Food, Supplies, Grooming			
MISCELLANEOUS			
Copies, Office Supplies			
Gifts, Cards			
Lottery			
Tithe, Donations			
TOTAL			
ATM WITHDRAWALS			
DEBIT CASH WITHDRAWALS			

THUR	FRI	SAT	SUN	TOTAL

MONTHLY MONEY JOURNAL

(Notes/Reflections/Insights/Progress)

Use these pages to jot down your thoughts and experiences with money as you go through the month.

Did you notice any spending patterns?

....

....

....

Are there consistent thoughts or feelings you noticed when spending at certain times or on specific items?

....

....

....

Were you surprised at how much you spent in certain areas?

....

....

....

Were you delighted to see how long your money lasted or how little you spent in some areas?

....

....

....

Have you come up with changes you want to make?

....

....

....

Other comments:

....

....

....

....

SPLURGE DIARY

Use these pages for those times when your spending is totally unplanned and way over budget. By recording your feelings and circumstances about a particular spending event you can begin to get in touch with some deeper reasons for spending.

Date	What I bought or spent money on	Amount	Cash	Charge
....	....	....	....	....
....	....	....	....	....
....	....	....	....	....
....	....	....	....	....

What happened right before the spending?

....

....

....

How was I feeling at that time?

....

....

....

How did I feel during the spending?

....

....

....

How did I feel a few hours later?

....

....

....

Sample feelings: *depressed, angry, excited, empty, lonely, guilty, shamed, remorseful, anxious, frantic, bored, nervous, powerful, deserving, noticed, confused, worried, fearful, hopeless, accepted, resentful, overwhelmed, tired, needy, disappointed*

How did I feel the next day and/or a week later?

....

....

....

What did I do as a result of that spending?

....

....

....

What did I learn about myself (my habits, feelings, patterns, thoughts)?

....

....

....

What unmet needs am I possibly trying to meet through my spending?

....

....

....

Who or what do these feelings remind me of from my past?

....

....

....

Next time, what can I do to replace the spending urge?
(See Alternative Activities List.)

....

....

....

Changes I've made since that spending:

....

....

....

Notes/Reflections/Insights:

VICTORY DIARY

Use these pages for those times when you *successfully did not give in* to your spending urges. Changing your spending patterns is a very positive and significant event, so acknowledge yourself on these occasions.

Date	What I *almost* bought or spent money on	Amount	Cash	Charge
....	....	....	....	....
....	....	....	....	....
....	....	....	....	....
....	....	....	....	....

What happened right before the spending urge?

....

....

....

How was I feeling at that time?

....

....

....

What did I do to *replace* the spending urge?

....

....

....

How did I feel immediately after deciding *not* to spend the money?

....

....

....

Sample feelings: *powerful, in charge, victorious, calm, relaxed, happy, proud, content, honest, satisfied, hopeful, validated, accepted, delighted, responsible, free*

How did I feel a few hours later?

....

....

....

How did I feel the next day and/or a week later?

....

....

....

What did I learn about myself (my habits, feelings, patterns, beliefs)?

....

....

....

I am proud of myself because:

....

....

....

How did I reward myself (praised myself, read a book, prepared a pleasant meal, took a nap, spent time on crafts or hobbies, took a drive, walked the dog, etc.)?

....

....

....

Notes/Reflections/Insights:

ALTERNATIVE ACTIVITIES LIST

For Replacing Spending Urges

Having the urge to spend, for some people, can be a very powerful feeling, so it is not easy to just *will it away.* When the urge comes up, you might try postponing it by engaging in another activity. I have listed some low-cost, no-cost activity ideas to help you gradually find ways to replace those urges with new, more positive behavior.

Try them out and see what works best for you. Your ideas are probably the most creative, so be sure to add many of your own.

These suggestions are especially effective if you are at the stage where you recognize you have behaviors and feelings associated with spending money. If your spending behavior has become much more serious and feels out of control, please see the Resource Guide in the back of the book for help.

Instead of spending at this particular time, I can . . .

✔ *Use the 24-hour technique: Tell yourself that you can buy this item. You can buy it tomorrow. You are choosing to wait 24 hours.*

✔ *Call a supportive friend or sponsor and talk about the events of the day and your feelings*

✔ *Take a walk or a drive, bike ride, hike, rollerblade or go to the gym*

✔ *Read a good story in a book or magazine*

✔ *Spend time on your favorite hobby or craft*

✔ *Watch a great movie*

✔ *Take in a museum, zoo or the botanical gardens*

✔ *Play with your children or your pets*

✔ *Have your partner give you a massage*

✔ *Take a bath or a nap*

✔ *Listen to music*

✔ *Meditate*

✔ *Now add your own*

My favorite activities to do or new things to try are:

....

....

....

....

....

MARCH

Questions to ponder when reviewing
finances or right before spending . . .

**Do I believe when I take out small amounts at the
ATM that I am really not spending as much money?**

How many times do I go to the ATM per week? Per day?

**How much would I save in service fees if I withdrew
larger amounts of ATM cash and made fewer
trips to the ATM?**

Would I be comfortable having that much cash on hand?

---

*"Tax time was very easy for us because of our habit of
tracking our spending. We always knew where the money was
going."*

After our boys were in school, I went back to work as a
home economics teacher. With my added income, there was
more money available and a greater need to better manage it.

We started a budget—not a real strict budget, but one that gave us guidelines.

I liked to track everything and break things down into categories. This helped keep priorities straight, like 10 percent tithing and making sure the house and car payments came first. And, my husband always believed in putting something away for emergencies. He put $100 a week into a savings bond and always wanted to make sure he provided something for me to fall back on.

In 1973, my husband had a heart attack and then later developed cancer. The daily radiation and medical costs were very expensive. It was a good thing we had a system for our finances so we had the money to cover these costs. We also managed to have money for all the children's health bills.

My husband always had his favorite sayings about money—"You have to handle money or it will handle you" and "If you don't have money to pay for something then you don't need it."

The keys to good money management for us were keeping track of where the money went and being disciplined. Both of us worked with our money and planned ahead and put money aside. My husband used to save coins in different cans—one can for each coin denomination. Our philosophy was "waste not, want not"—one that we grew up with during the Depression when we didn't waste anything. Those years left an impact on us. And throughout our lives, we were always satisfied with simple things and didn't care for very luxurious, expensive things.

Now I'm proud to say my children also are doing very well with money.

Marjorie Willis, Emmett, Idaho
Retired, Age 75
Two Children, Ages 55 and 53

MARCH WEEK OF: _____

HOME	MON	TUES	WED
Groceries			
Meals Out			
Snacks, Beverages, Liquor			
Supplies, Furnishings			
TRANSPORTATION			
Gas, Public Transportation			
Vehicle Expense			
PERSONAL CARE			
Clothing, Accessories			
Laundry, Shoe Care			
Hair Care, Toiletries			
Nails, Massage			
ENTERTAINMENT			
Movies, Videos			
CDs, Books			
Hobbies, Sports, Gym			
HEALTH CARE			
Prescriptions, Supplements			
Doctors, Dentists			
CHILDREN			
Child Care, Sitter			
Allowance, School Expense			
PETS			
Food, Supplies, Grooming			
MISCELLANEOUS			
Copies, Office Supplies			
Gifts, Cards			
Lottery			
Tithe, Donations			
TOTAL			
ATM WITHDRAWALS			
DEBIT CASH WITHDRAWALS			

THUR	FRI	SAT	SUN	TOTAL

MARCH WEEK OF: _____

HOME	MON	TUES	WED
Groceries			
Meals Out			
Snacks, Beverages, Liquor			
Supplies, Furnishings			
TRANSPORTATION			
Gas, Public Transportation			
Vehicle Expense			
PERSONAL CARE			
Clothing, Accessories			
Laundry, Shoe Care			
Hair Care, Toiletries			
Nails, Massage			
ENTERTAINMENT			
Movies, Videos			
CDs, Books			
Hobbies, Sports, Gym			
HEALTH CARE			
Prescriptions, Supplements			
Doctors, Dentists			
CHILDREN			
Child Care, Sitter			
Allowance, School Expense			
PETS			
Food, Supplies, Grooming			
MISCELLANEOUS			
Copies, Office Supplies			
Gifts, Cards			
Lottery			
Tithe, Donations			
TOTAL			
ATM WITHDRAWALS			
DEBIT CASH WITHDRAWALS			

THUR	FRI	SAT	SUN	TOTAL

MARCH   WEEK OF: _____

HOME	MON	TUES	WED
Groceries			
Meals Out			
Snacks, Beverages, Liquor			
Supplies, Furnishings			
TRANSPORTATION			
Gas, Public Transportation			
Vehicle Expense			
PERSONAL CARE			
Clothing, Accessories			
Laundry, Shoe Care			
Hair Care, Toiletries			
Nails, Massage			
ENTERTAINMENT			
Movies, Videos			
CDs, Books			
Hobbies, Sports, Gym			
HEALTH CARE			
Prescriptions, Supplements			
Doctors, Dentists			
CHILDREN			
Child Care, Sitter			
Allowance, School Expense			
PETS			
Food, Supplies, Grooming			
MISCELLANEOUS			
Copies, Office Supplies			
Gifts, Cards			
Lottery			
Tithe, Donations			
TOTAL			
ATM WITHDRAWALS			
DEBIT CASH WITHDRAWALS			

THUR	FRI	SAT	SUN	TOTAL

MARCH WEEK OF: _____

HOME	MON	TUES	WED
Groceries			
Meals Out			
Snacks, Beverages, Liquor			
Supplies, Furnishings			
TRANSPORTATION			
Gas, Public Transportation			
Vehicle Expense			
PERSONAL CARE			
Clothing, Accessories			
Laundry, Shoe Care			
Hair Care, Toiletries			
Nails, Massage			
ENTERTAINMENT			
Movies, Videos			
CDs, Books			
Hobbies, Sports, Gym			
HEALTH CARE			
Prescriptions, Supplements			
Doctors, Dentists			
CHILDREN			
Child Care, Sitter			
Allowance, School Expense			
PETS			
Food, Supplies, Grooming			
MISCELLANEOUS			
Copies, Office Supplies			
Gifts, Cards			
Lottery			
Tithe, Donations			
TOTAL			
ATM WITHDRAWALS			
DEBIT CASH WITHDRAWALS			

THUR	FRI	SAT	SUN	TOTAL

MARCH WEEK OF: _____

HOME	MON	TUES	WED
Groceries			
Meals Out			
Snacks, Beverages, Liquor			
Supplies, Furnishings			
TRANSPORTATION			
Gas, Public Transportation			
Vehicle Expense			
PERSONAL CARE			
Clothing, Accessories			
Laundry, Shoe Care			
Hair Care, Toiletries			
Nails, Massage			
ENTERTAINMENT			
Movies, Videos			
CDs, Books			
Hobbies, Sports, Gym			
HEALTH CARE			
Prescriptions, Supplements			
Doctors, Dentists			
CHILDREN			
Child Care, Sitter			
Allowance, School Expense			
PETS			
Food, Supplies, Grooming			
MISCELLANEOUS			
Copies, Office Supplies			
Gifts, Cards			
Lottery			
Tithe, Donations			
TOTAL			
ATM WITHDRAWALS			
DEBIT CASH WITHDRAWALS			

THUR	FRI	SAT	SUN	TOTAL

MONTHLY MONEY JOURNAL

(Notes/Reflections/Insights/Progress)

Use these pages to jot down your thoughts and experiences with money as you go through the month.

Did you notice any spending patterns?

....

....

....

Are there consistent thoughts or feelings you noticed when spending at certain times or on specific items?

....

....

....

Were you surprised at how much you spent in certain areas?

....

....

....

Were you delighted to see how long your money lasted or how little you spent in some areas?

....

....

....

Have you come up with changes you want to make?

....

....

....

Other comments:

....

....

....

....

SPLURGE DIARY

Use these pages for those times when your spending is totally unplanned and way over budget. By recording your feelings and circumstances about a particular spending event you can begin to get in touch with some deeper reasons for spending.

Date	What I bought or spent money on	Amount	Cash	Charge
....	....	....	....	....
....	....	....	....	....
....	....	....	....	....
....	....	....	....	....

What happened right before the spending?

....

....

....

How was I feeling at that time?

....

....

....

How did I feel during the spending?

....

....

....

How did I feel a few hours later?

....

....

....

Sample feelings: *depressed, angry, excited, empty, lonely, guilty, shamed, remorseful, anxious, frantic, bored, nervous, powerful, deserving, noticed, confused, worried, fearful, hopeless, accepted, resentful, overwhelmed, tired, needy, disappointed*

How did I feel the next day and/or a week later?

....

....

....

What did I do as a result of that spending?

....

....

....

What did I learn about myself (my habits, feelings, patterns, thoughts)?

....

....

....

What unmet needs am I possibly trying to meet through my spending?

....

....

....

Who or what do these feelings remind me of from my past?

....

....

....

Next time, what can I do to replace the spending urge?
(See Alternative Activities List.)

....

....

....

Changes I've made since that spending:

....

....

....

Notes/Reflections/Insights:

VICTORY DIARY

Use these pages for those times when you *successfully did not give in* to your spending urges. Changing your spending patterns is a very positive and significant event, so acknowledge yourself on these occasions.

Date	What I *almost* bought or spent money on	Amount	Cash	Charge
....	....	....	....	....
....	....	....	....	....
....	....	....	....	....
....	....	....	....	....

What happened right before the spending urge?

....

....

....

How was I feeling at that time?

....

....

....

What did I do to *replace* the spending urge?

....

....

....

How did I feel immediately after deciding *not* to spend the money?

....

....

....

Sample feelings: *powerful, in charge, victorious, calm, relaxed, happy, proud, content, honest, satisfied, hopeful, validated, accepted, delighted, responsible, free*

How did I feel a few hours later?

....

....

....

How did I feel the next day and/or a week later?

....

....

....

What did I learn about myself (my habits, feelings, patterns, beliefs)?

....

....

....

I am proud of myself because:

....

....

....

How did I reward myself (praised myself, read a book, prepared a pleasant meal, took a nap, spent time on crafts or hobbies, took a drive, walked the dog, etc.)?

....

....

....

Notes/Reflections/Insights:

ALTERNATIVE ACTIVITIES LIST

For Replacing Spending Urges

Having the urge to spend, for some people, can be a very powerful feeling, so it is not easy to just *will it away*. When the urge comes up, you might try postponing it by engaging in another activity. I have listed some low-cost, no-cost activity ideas to help you gradually find ways to replace those urges with new, more positive behavior.

Try them out and see what works best for you. Your ideas are probably the most creative, so be sure to add many of your own.

These suggestions are especially effective if you are at the stage where you recognize you have behaviors and feelings associated with spending money. If your spending behavior has become much more serious and feels out of control, please see the Resource Guide in the back of the book for help.

Instead of spending at this particular time, I can . . .

✔ *Use the 24-hour technique: Tell yourself that you can buy this item. You can buy it tomorrow. You are choosing to wait 24 hours.*

- *Call a supportive friend or sponsor and talk about the events of the day and your feelings*

- *Take a walk or a drive, bike ride, hike, rollerblade or go to the gym*

- *Read a good story in a book or magazine*

- *Spend time on your favorite hobby or craft*

- *Watch a great movie*

- *Take in a museum, zoo or the botanical gardens*

- *Play with your children or your pets*

- *Have your partner give you a massage*

- *Take a bath or a nap*

- *Listen to music*

- *Meditate*

- *Now add your own*

My favorite activities to do or new things to try are:

....

....

....

....

....

APRIL

Questions to ponder when reviewing
finances or right before spending . . .

**What can I do this year to make tax preparation
easier and less stressful next year?**

**Have I noticed if I spend more money during any
particular times or days (payday, weekends, with the
children, without the children, with particular
friends, noon hour, certain times of the month,
full moon . . . add your own)?**

**What extra summer expenses are coming up?
Have I started saving for them?**

---

*"There is no substitute for money when you need it. All
the dresses or electronic equipment in the world won't help
you if you lose a job."*

In the beginning, we used to fight about money a lot. Now,
after being married ten years, we don't fight about it anymore.
We can explain all of our purchases and spending through our

records and don't have to argue over imaginary spending we each thought the other was doing.

We have learned how much a little bit here and there adds up. To see it on paper makes such a difference. Daily money like the $2 for a big Coke really adds up over ten years. Then we started realizing how we could have saved that money. The more we do this, the more it adds up and just snowballs.

With both of us working away from home, we realized we stopped a lot at fast-food places. Soon we found that it was much cheaper to bring our food to work, since we were spending about $4 to $5 a day on those quick meals. In fact, I was able to fund my IRA by brown-bagging.

Another change was to not go out for big meals anymore. Instead, we just have a cappuccino and dessert and still enjoy the experience of going out. Often, we go to the bookstore with our children. They are old enough to go off looking at books, and we get to take a break and have coffee and dessert together. We save the cost of a high-priced meal and a baby-sitter.

By monitoring our spending, we have paid off our credit cards and don't have bills anymore. It's a great feeling. It's actually strange when the mail comes and there are no bills.

The more I save, the more I am inspired—I see results and have security. When I see money in my savings account, it is such a thrill. There is no feeling like it!

In the last seven years, we went from saving 3 to 5 to 10 percent of our income and now we save 15 percent—and we haven't missed that money.

The key is keeping track of spending. I can see it in black and white. I see what I am accomplishing from year to year and it makes me realize what I am doing is all worthwhile.

Donna Groom, Fountain Hills, Ariz.
Registered Nurse, Age 41
Two Children, Ages 5 and 8

APRIL WEEK OF: _____

HOME	MON	TUES	WED
Groceries			
Meals Out			
Snacks, Beverages, Liquor			
Supplies, Furnishings			
TRANSPORTATION			
Gas, Public Transportation			
Vehicle Expense			
PERSONAL CARE			
Clothing, Accessories			
Laundry, Shoe Care			
Hair Care, Toiletries			
Nails, Massage			
ENTERTAINMENT			
Movies, Videos			
CDs, Books			
Hobbies, Sports, Gym			
HEALTH CARE			
Prescriptions, Supplements			
Doctors, Dentists			
CHILDREN			
Child Care, Sitter			
Allowance, School Expense			
PETS			
Food, Supplies, Grooming			
MISCELLANEOUS			
Copies, Office Supplies			
Gifts, Cards			
Lottery			
Tithe, Donations			
TOTAL			
ATM WITHDRAWALS			
DEBIT CASH WITHDRAWALS			

THUR	FRI	SAT	SUN	TOTAL

APRIL WEEK OF: _____

HOME	MON	TUES	WED
Groceries			
Meals Out			
Snacks, Beverages, Liquor			
Supplies, Furnishings			
TRANSPORTATION			
Gas, Public Transportation			
Vehicle Expense			
PERSONAL CARE			
Clothing, Accessories			
Laundry, Shoe Care			
Hair Care, Toiletries			
Nails, Massage			
ENTERTAINMENT			
Movies, Videos			
CDs, Books			
Hobbies, Sports, Gym			
HEALTH CARE			
Prescriptions, Supplements			
Doctors, Dentists			
CHILDREN			
Child Care, Sitter			
Allowance, School Expense			
PETS			
Food, Supplies, Grooming			
MISCELLANEOUS			
Copies, Office Supplies			
Gifts, Cards			
Lottery			
Tithe, Donations			
TOTAL			
ATM WITHDRAWALS			
DEBIT CASH WITHDRAWALS			

THUR	FRI	SAT	SUN	TOTAL

APRIL   WEEK OF: _____

HOME	MON	TUES	WED
Groceries			
Meals Out			
Snacks, Beverages, Liquor			
Supplies, Furnishings			
TRANSPORTATION			
Gas, Public Transportation			
Vehicle Expense			
PERSONAL CARE			
Clothing, Accessories			
Laundry, Shoe Care			
Hair Care, Toiletries			
Nails, Massage			
ENTERTAINMENT			
Movies, Videos			
CDs, Books			
Hobbies, Sports, Gym			
HEALTH CARE			
Prescriptions, Supplements			
Doctors, Dentists			
CHILDREN			
Child Care, Sitter			
Allowance, School Expense			
PETS			
Food, Supplies, Grooming			
MISCELLANEOUS			
Copies, Office Supplies			
Gifts, Cards			
Lottery			
Tithe, Donations			
TOTAL			
ATM WITHDRAWALS			
DEBIT CASH WITHDRAWALS			

THUR	FRI	SAT	SUN	TOTAL

APRIL WEEK OF: _____

HOME	MON	TUES	WED
Groceries			
Meals Out			
Snacks, Beverages, Liquor			
Supplies, Furnishings			
TRANSPORTATION			
Gas, Public Transportation			
Vehicle Expense			
PERSONAL CARE			
Clothing, Accessories			
Laundry, Shoe Care			
Hair Care, Toiletries			
Nails, Massage			
ENTERTAINMENT			
Movies, Videos			
CDs, Books			
Hobbies, Sports, Gym			
HEALTH CARE			
Prescriptions, Supplements			
Doctors, Dentists			
CHILDREN			
Child Care, Sitter			
Allowance, School Expense			
PETS			
Food, Supplies, Grooming			
MISCELLANEOUS			
Copies, Office Supplies			
Gifts, Cards			
Lottery			
Tithe, Donations			
TOTAL			
ATM WITHDRAWALS			
DEBIT CASH WITHDRAWALS			

THUR	FRI	SAT	SUN	TOTAL

APRIL   WEEK OF: _____

HOME	MON	TUES	WED
Groceries			
Meals Out			
Snacks, Beverages, Liquor			
Supplies, Furnishings			
TRANSPORTATION			
Gas, Public Transportation			
Vehicle Expense			
PERSONAL CARE			
Clothing, Accessories			
Laundry, Shoe Care			
Hair Care, Toiletries			
Nails, Massage			
ENTERTAINMENT			
Movies, Videos			
CDs, Books			
Hobbies, Sports, Gym			
HEALTH CARE			
Prescriptions, Supplements			
Doctors, Dentists			
CHILDREN			
Child Care, Sitter			
Allowance, School Expense			
PETS			
Food, Supplies, Grooming			
MISCELLANEOUS			
Copies, Office Supplies			
Gifts, Cards			
Lottery			
Tithe, Donations			
TOTAL			
ATM WITHDRAWALS			
DEBIT CASH WITHDRAWALS			

THUR	FRI	SAT	SUN	TOTAL

MONTHLY MONEY JOURNAL

(Notes/Reflections/Insights/Progress)

Use these pages to jot down your thoughts and experiences with money as you go through the month.

Did you notice any spending patterns?

....

....

....

Are there consistent thoughts or feelings you noticed when spending at certain times or on specific items?

....

....

....

Were you surprised at how much you spent in certain areas?

....

....

....

Were you delighted to see how long your money lasted or how little you spent in some areas?

....

....

....

Have you come up with changes you want to make?

....

....

....

Other comments:

....

....

....

....

SPLURGE DIARY

Use these pages for those times when your spending is totally unplanned and way over budget. By recording your feelings and circumstances about a particular spending event you can begin to get in touch with some deeper reasons for spending.

Date	What I bought or spent money on	Amount	Cash	Charge
....	....	....	....	....
....	....	....	....	....
....	....	....	....	....
....	....	....	....	....

What happened right before the spending?

....

....

....

How was I feeling at that time?

....

....

....

How did I feel during the spending?

....

....

....

How did I feel a few hours later?

....

....

....

Sample feelings: *depressed, angry, excited, empty, lonely, guilty, shamed, remorseful, anxious, frantic, bored, nervous, powerful, deserving, noticed, confused, worried, fearful, hopeless, accepted, resentful, overwhelmed, tired, needy, disappointed*

How did I feel the next day and/or a week later?

....

....

....

What did I do as a result of that spending?

....

....

....

What did I learn about myself (my habits, feelings, patterns, thoughts)?

....

....

....

What unmet needs am I possibly trying to meet through my spending?

....

....

....

Who or what do these feelings remind me of from my past?

....

....

....

Next time, what can I do to replace the spending urge?
(See Alternative Activities List.)

....

....

....

Changes I've made since that spending:

....

....

....

Notes/Reflections/Insights:

VICTORY DIARY

Use these pages for those times when you *successfully did not give in* to your spending urges. Changing your spending patterns is a very positive and significant event, so acknowledge yourself on these occasions.

Date	What I *almost* bought or spent money on	Amount	Cash	Charge
....	....	....	....	....
....	....	....	....	....
....	....	....	....	....
....	....	....	....	....

What happened right before the spending urge?

....

....

....

How was I feeling at that time?

....

....

....

What did I do to *replace* the spending urge?

....

....

....

How did I feel immediately after deciding *not* to spend the money?

....

....

....

Sample feelings: *powerful, in charge, victorious, calm, relaxed, happy, proud, content, honest, satisfied, hopeful, validated, accepted, delighted, responsible, free*

How did I feel a few hours later?

....

....

....

How did I feel the next day and/or a week later?

....

....

....

What did I learn about myself (my habits, feelings, patterns, beliefs)?

....

....

....

I am proud of myself because:

....

....

....

How did I reward myself (praised myself, read a book, prepared a pleasant meal, took a nap, spent time on crafts or hobbies, took a drive, walked the dog, etc.)?

....

....

....

Notes/Reflections/Insights:

ALTERNATIVE ACTIVITIES LIST

For Replacing Spending Urges

Having the urge to spend, for some people, can be a very powerful feeling, so it is not easy to just *will it away*. When the urge comes up, you might try postponing it by engaging in another activity. I have listed some low-cost, no-cost activity ideas to help you gradually find ways to replace those urges with new, more positive behavior.

Try them out and see what works best for you. Your ideas are probably the most creative, so be sure to add many of your own.

These suggestions are especially effective if you are at the stage where you recognize you have behaviors and feelings associated with spending money. If your spending behavior has become much more serious and feels out of control, please see the Resource Guide in the back of the book for help.

Instead of spending at this particular time, I can . . .

✔ *Use the 24-hour technique: Tell yourself that you can buy this item. You can buy it tomorrow. You are choosing to wait 24 hours.*

- ✔ *Call a supportive friend or sponsor and talk about the events of the day and your feelings*

- ✔ *Take a walk or a drive, bike ride, hike, rollerblade or go to the gym*

- ✔ *Read a good story in a book or magazine*

- ✔ *Spend time on your favorite hobby or craft*

- ✔ *Watch a great movie*

- ✔ *Take in a museum, zoo or the botanical gardens*

- ✔ *Play with your children or your pets*

- ✔ *Have your partner give you a massage*

- ✔ *Take a bath or a nap*

- ✔ *Listen to music*

- ✔ *Meditate*

- ✔ *Now add your own*

My favorite activities to do or new things to try are:

....

....

....

....

....

MAY

Questions to ponder when reviewing
finances or right before spending . . .

**Do I get satisfaction from buying something at a
great discount even if I don't really need it?**

**Is this money really extra money or is it part of
the money I will be needing for some upcoming
expenses this month (like utilities, haircut,
baby-sitter, credit card payment)?**

What will happen if I don't buy this item?

---

*"I find it to be an enjoyable challenge to still do what we
want to do and also be able to do things with our three boys. We
keep it simple, have fun and have no sense of deprivation."*

When we started recording our expenses and breaking down
everything into separate categories, it helped us to see how we
could cut back. Now we are conscious of how little things add
up and make such a difference.

We saw we were going to dinner four times a month and
decided to cut back to two times a month. We saved $200. On

the other two evenings, we usually rent a movie and spend time at home instead.

After we monitored our grocery bills, we decided also to cut back our grocery spending. We now shop only once a week and have a spending limit of $150 a week for five. We saved $200 a month with this strategy. With that savings, we plan to make a down payment on a new car next year and apply the $200 savings to the monthly payment.

I enjoy having the ability to forecast expenses. I can go through each month and see what we spent, and can anticipate those expenses for future months. If I see a high expense coming three months in advance—like insurance, school or Christmas—I can prepare for it. It makes a big difference to be able to plan ahead for these expenses.

Looking at the big picture versus one piece of it is important to me. When I get an overall snapshot of the expenses, I can see where to make adjustments. My wife and I do this together. Every Sunday night when the kids are in bed, we sit down and talk about the finances. We make decisions about expenses and decide if we should spend money on something or save it. We plan ahead by looking at our schedules for the week and determine who will do what; for instance, which one of us will shop for groceries on Thursday.

Before we started using a budget book and tracking expenses, we probably saved less than 5 percent of our income. We now save about 10 to 15 percent—even with three kids and my wife staying at home. There is discipline involved, but after tracking expenses for a period of time we started to look forward to it. Later, we set goals and planned to get what we set out to get. That's rewarding.

Albert and Ginny Flores, Des Plaines, Ill.
Xerox Marketing Manager, Ages 37 and 38
Three Children, Ages 3, 4 and 7

MAY WEEK OF: _____

HOME	MON	TUES	WED
Groceries			
Meals Out			
Snacks, Beverages, Liquor			
Supplies, Furnishings			
TRANSPORTATION			
Gas, Public Transportation			
Vehicle Expense			
PERSONAL CARE			
Clothing, Accessories			
Laundry, Shoe Care			
Hair Care, Toiletries			
Nails, Massage			
ENTERTAINMENT			
Movies, Videos			
CDs, Books			
Hobbies, Sports, Gym			
HEALTH CARE			
Prescriptions, Supplements			
Doctors, Dentists			
CHILDREN			
Child Care, Sitter			
Allowance, School Expense			
PETS			
Food, Supplies, Grooming			
MISCELLANEOUS			
Copies, Office Supplies			
Gifts, Cards			
Lottery			
Tithe, Donations			
TOTAL			
ATM WITHDRAWALS			
DEBIT CASH WITHDRAWALS			

THUR	FRI	SAT	SUN	TOTAL

MAY   WEEK OF: _____

HOME	MON	TUES	WED
Groceries			
Meals Out			
Snacks, Beverages, Liquor			
Supplies, Furnishings			
TRANSPORTATION			
Gas, Public Transportation			
Vehicle Expense			
PERSONAL CARE			
Clothing, Accessories			
Laundry, Shoe Care			
Hair Care, Toiletries			
Nails, Massage			
ENTERTAINMENT			
Movies, Videos			
CDs, Books			
Hobbies, Sports, Gym			
HEALTH CARE			
Prescriptions, Supplements			
Doctors, Dentists			
CHILDREN			
Child Care, Sitter			
Allowance, School Expense			
PETS			
Food, Supplies, Grooming			
MISCELLANEOUS			
Copies, Office Supplies			
Gifts, Cards			
Lottery			
Tithe, Donations			
TOTAL			
ATM WITHDRAWALS			
DEBIT CASH WITHDRAWALS			

THUR	FRI	SAT	SUN	TOTAL

MAY WEEK OF: _____

HOME	MON	TUES	WED
Groceries			
Meals Out			
Snacks, Beverages, Liquor			
Supplies, Furnishings			
TRANSPORTATION			
Gas, Public Transportation			
Vehicle Expense			
PERSONAL CARE			
Clothing, Accessories			
Laundry, Shoe Care			
Hair Care, Toiletries			
Nails, Massage			
ENTERTAINMENT			
Movies, Videos			
CDs, Books			
Hobbies, Sports, Gym			
HEALTH CARE			
Prescriptions, Supplements			
Doctors, Dentists			
CHILDREN			
Child Care, Sitter			
Allowance, School Expense			
PETS			
Food, Supplies, Grooming			
MISCELLANEOUS			
Copies, Office Supplies			
Gifts, Cards			
Lottery			
Tithe, Donations			
TOTAL			
ATM WITHDRAWALS			
DEBIT CASH WITHDRAWALS			

THUR	FRI	SAT	SUN	TOTAL

MAY WEEK OF: _____

HOME	MON	TUES	WED
Groceries			
Meals Out			
Snacks, Beverages, Liquor			
Supplies, Furnishings			
TRANSPORTATION			
Gas, Public Transportation			
Vehicle Expense			
PERSONAL CARE			
Clothing, Accessories			
Laundry, Shoe Care			
Hair Care, Toiletries			
Nails, Massage			
ENTERTAINMENT			
Movies, Videos			
CDs, Books			
Hobbies, Sports, Gym			
HEALTH CARE			
Prescriptions, Supplements			
Doctors, Dentists			
CHILDREN			
Child Care, Sitter			
Allowance, School Expense			
PETS			
Food, Supplies, Grooming			
MISCELLANEOUS			
Copies, Office Supplies			
Gifts, Cards			
Lottery			
Tithe, Donations			
TOTAL			
ATM WITHDRAWALS			
DEBIT CASH WITHDRAWALS			

THUR	FRI	SAT	SUN	TOTAL

MAY WEEK OF: _____

HOME	MON	TUES	WED
Groceries			
Meals Out			
Snacks, Beverages, Liquor			
Supplies, Furnishings			
TRANSPORTATION			
Gas, Public Transportation			
Vehicle Expense			
PERSONAL CARE			
Clothing, Accessories			
Laundry, Shoe Care			
Hair Care, Toiletries			
Nails, Massage			
ENTERTAINMENT			
Movies, Videos			
CDs, Books			
Hobbies, Sports, Gym			
HEALTH CARE			
Prescriptions, Supplements			
Doctors, Dentists			
CHILDREN			
Child Care, Sitter			
Allowance, School Expense			
PETS			
Food, Supplies, Grooming			
MISCELLANEOUS			
Copies, Office Supplies			
Gifts, Cards			
Lottery			
Tithe, Donations			
TOTAL			
ATM WITHDRAWALS			
DEBIT CASH WITHDRAWALS			

THUR	FRI	SAT	SUN	TOTAL

MONTHLY MONEY JOURNAL

(Notes/Reflections/Insights/Progress)

Use these pages to jot down your thoughts and experiences with money as you go through the month.

Did you notice any spending patterns?

....

....

....

Are there consistent thoughts or feelings you noticed when spending at certain times or on specific items?

....

....

....

Were you surprised at how much you spent in certain areas?

....

....

....

Were you delighted to see how long your money lasted or how little you spent in some areas?

....

....

....

Have you come up with changes you want to make?

....

....

....

Other comments:

....

....

....

....

SPLURGE DIARY

Use these pages for those times when your spending is totally unplanned and way over budget. By recording your feelings and circumstances about a particular spending event you can begin to get in touch with some deeper reasons for spending.

Date	What I bought or spent money on	Amount	Cash	Charge
....	....	....	....	....
....	....	....	....	....
....	....	....	....	....
....	....	....	....	....

What happened right before the spending?

....

....

....

How was I feeling at that time?

....

....

....

How did I feel during the spending?

....

....

....

How did I feel a few hours later?

....

....

....

Sample feelings: *depressed, angry, excited, empty, lonely, guilty, shamed, remorseful, anxious, frantic, bored, nervous, powerful, deserving, noticed, confused, worried, fearful, hopeless, accepted, resentful, overwhelmed, tired, needy, disappointed*

How did I feel the next day and/or a week later?

....

....

....

What did I do as a result of that spending?

....

....

....

What did I learn about myself (my habits, feelings, patterns, thoughts)?

....

....

....

What unmet needs am I possibly trying to meet through my spending?

....

....

....

Who or what do these feelings remind me of from my past?

....

....

....

Next time, what can I do to replace the spending urge?
(See Alternative Activities List.)

....

....

....

Changes I've made since that spending:

....

....

....

Notes/Reflections/Insights:

VICTORY DIARY

Use these pages for those times when you *successfully did not give in* to your spending urges. Changing your spending patterns is a very positive and significant event, so acknowledge yourself on these occasions.

Date	What I *almost* bought or spent money on	Amount	Cash	Charge
....	....	....	....	....
....	....	....	....	....
....	....	....	....	....
....	....	....	....	....

What happened right before the spending urge?

....

....

....

How was I feeling at that time?

....

....

....

What did I do to *replace* the spending urge?

....

....

....

How did I feel immediately after deciding *not* to spend the money?

....

....

....

Sample feelings: *powerful, in charge, victorious, calm, relaxed, happy, proud, content, honest, satisfied, hopeful, validated, accepted, delighted, responsible, free*

How did I feel a few hours later?

....

....

....

How did I feel the next day and/or a week later?

....

....

....

What did I learn about myself (my habits, feelings, patterns, beliefs)?

....

....

....

I am proud of myself because:

....

....

....

How did I reward myself (praised myself, read a book, prepared a pleasant meal, took a nap, spent time on crafts or hobbies, took a drive, walked the dog, etc.)?

....

....

....

Notes/Reflections/Insights:

ALTERNATIVE ACTIVITIES LIST

For Replacing Spending Urges

Having the urge to spend, for some people, can be a very powerful feeling, so it is not easy to just *will it away.* When the urge comes up, you might try postponing it by engaging in another activity. I have listed some low-cost, no-cost activity ideas to help you gradually find ways to replace those urges with new, more positive behavior.

Try them out and see what works best for you. Your ideas are probably the most creative, so be sure to add many of your own.

These suggestions are especially effective if you are at the stage where you recognize you have behaviors and feelings associated with spending money. If your spending behavior has become much more serious and feels out of control, please see the Resource Guide in the back of the book for help.

Instead of spending at this particular time, I can . . .

✔ *Use the 24-hour technique: Tell yourself that you can buy this item. You can buy it tomorrow. You are choosing to wait 24 hours.*

- *Call a supportive friend or sponsor and talk about the events of the day and your feelings*

- *Take a walk or a drive, bike ride, hike, rollerblade or go to the gym*

- *Read a good story in a book or magazine*

- *Spend time on your favorite hobby or craft*

- *Watch a great movie*

- *Take in a museum, zoo or the botanical gardens*

- *Play with your children or your pets*

- *Have your partner give you a massage*

- *Take a bath or a nap*

- *Listen to music*

- *Meditate*

- *Now add your own*

My favorite activities to do or new things to try are:

....

....

....

....

....

JUNE

Questions to ponder when reviewing
finances or right before spending . . .

**Do I justify my spending because it is for my
children or someone else and not for me?**

**How could I creatively satisfy my own or my family's
needs and desires without spending as much money?**

**On vacation, will this souvenir mean as much
to me back home as it does here?**

---

*"When my husband and I were married, we had more debt
than income. Soon we developed a plan we both could agree on
to attack our debt. Within two years, we were debt-free."*

When my husband and I were first married, we brought an
accumulation of debt that far exceeded our income level. Our
expenditures seemed to leave no room for savings or anything
else.

I ran across the book *Common Cent$* (now *The Budget
Kit*) and hoped to organize a plan to control our finances. We

followed the book exactly, outlining all of our income and expenditures. We developed a plan we both agreed on, kept track of *all* of our spending and made major adjustments in our spending habits. A lot of sacrifices were necessary, but we were able to see the rewards by sticking to our goals. Within two years, we were debt-free.

Four years later, our financial situation seems very similar to what it was when we were first married. The only difference is that now we have a higher income, a house, three children and more credit than we could possibly need. We have fallen into "the more you make, the more you spend" trap.

We lost most of our control through the lack of financial communication. We both bought impulsively without discussing whether or not we needed it or if we could really afford it. Because we had credit and we were making more money, I think we both became disillusioned. One month we would try to play catch up and not spend. The next month we would reward ourselves and spend money.

Because our plan worked so well in the past, we are again using the budget book and reapplying the steps to regain control of our financial situation. The first step we took was a consolidation loan for the credit card debt. We then cancelled all the credit cards except for one, in case of emergency.

These are five goals my husband and I are working towards (lessons learned!): (1) As your income level grows, try to live at the previous income level. (2) Save the difference. (3) Don't spend money you don't have, even though you know more money is on the way. (4) Always keep track of your exact expenditures and why you made them. (5) Save ahead for purchases and don't use credit.

Michele and Todd Brigham, Dallas, Texas
Restaurant General Manager, Ages 32 and 30
Three Children, Ages 6, 4 and 2

JUNE WEEK OF: _____

HOME	MON	TUES	WED
Groceries			
Meals Out			
Snacks, Beverages, Liquor			
Supplies, Furnishings			
TRANSPORTATION			
Gas, Public Transportation			
Vehicle Expense			
PERSONAL CARE			
Clothing, Accessories			
Laundry, Shoe Care			
Hair Care, Toiletries			
Nails, Massage			
ENTERTAINMENT			
Movies, Videos			
CDs, Books			
Hobbies, Sports, Gym			
HEALTH CARE			
Prescriptions, Supplements			
Doctors, Dentists			
CHILDREN			
Child Care, Sitter			
Allowance, School Expense			
PETS			
Food, Supplies, Grooming			
MISCELLANEOUS			
Copies, Office Supplies			
Gifts, Cards			
Lottery			
Tithe, Donations			
TOTAL			
ATM WITHDRAWALS			
DEBIT CASH WITHDRAWALS			

THUR	FRI	SAT	SUN	TOTAL

JUNE WEEK OF: _____

HOME	MON	TUES	WED
Groceries			
Meals Out			
Snacks, Beverages, Liquor			
Supplies, Furnishings			
TRANSPORTATION			
Gas, Public Transportation			
Vehicle Expense			
PERSONAL CARE			
Clothing, Accessories			
Laundry, Shoe Care			
Hair Care, Toiletries			
Nails, Massage			
ENTERTAINMENT			
Movies, Videos			
CDs, Books			
Hobbies, Sports, Gym			
HEALTH CARE			
Prescriptions, Supplements			
Doctors, Dentists			
CHILDREN			
Child Care, Sitter			
Allowance, School Expense			
PETS			
Food, Supplies, Grooming			
MISCELLANEOUS			
Copies, Office Supplies			
Gifts, Cards			
Lottery			
Tithe, Donations			
TOTAL			
ATM WITHDRAWALS			
DEBIT CASH WITHDRAWALS			

THUR	FRI	SAT	SUN	TOTAL

JUNE WEEK OF: _____

HOME	MON	TUES	WED
Groceries			
Meals Out			
Snacks, Beverages, Liquor			
Supplies, Furnishings			
TRANSPORTATION			
Gas, Public Transportation			
Vehicle Expense			
PERSONAL CARE			
Clothing, Accessories			
Laundry, Shoe Care			
Hair Care, Toiletries			
Nails, Massage			
ENTERTAINMENT			
Movies, Videos			
CDs, Books			
Hobbies, Sports, Gym			
HEALTH CARE			
Prescriptions, Supplements			
Doctors, Dentists			
CHILDREN			
Child Care, Sitter			
Allowance, School Expense			
PETS			
Food, Supplies, Grooming			
MISCELLANEOUS			
Copies, Office Supplies			
Gifts, Cards			
Lottery			
Tithe, Donations			
TOTAL			
ATM WITHDRAWALS			
DEBIT CASH WITHDRAWALS			

THUR	FRI	SAT	SUN	TOTAL

JUNE   WEEK OF: _____

HOME	MON	TUES	WED
Groceries			
Meals Out			
Snacks, Beverages, Liquor			
Supplies, Furnishings			
TRANSPORTATION			
Gas, Public Transportation			
Vehicle Expense			
PERSONAL CARE			
Clothing, Accessories			
Laundry, Shoe Care			
Hair Care, Toiletries			
Nails, Massage			
ENTERTAINMENT			
Movies, Videos			
CDs, Books			
Hobbies, Sports, Gym			
HEALTH CARE			
Prescriptions, Supplements			
Doctors, Dentists			
CHILDREN			
Child Care, Sitter			
Allowance, School Expense			
PETS			
Food, Supplies, Grooming			
MISCELLANEOUS			
Copies, Office Supplies			
Gifts, Cards			
Lottery			
Tithe, Donations			
TOTAL			
ATM WITHDRAWALS			
DEBIT CASH WITHDRAWALS			

THUR	FRI	SAT	SUN	TOTAL

JUNE WEEK OF: _____

HOME	MON	TUES	WED
Groceries			
Meals Out			
Snacks, Beverages, Liquor			
Supplies, Furnishings			
TRANSPORTATION			
Gas, Public Transportation			
Vehicle Expense			
PERSONAL CARE			
Clothing, Accessories			
Laundry, Shoe Care			
Hair Care, Toiletries			
Nails, Massage			
ENTERTAINMENT			
Movies, Videos			
CDs, Books			
Hobbies, Sports, Gym			
HEALTH CARE			
Prescriptions, Supplements			
Doctors, Dentists			
CHILDREN			
Child Care, Sitter			
Allowance, School Expense			
PETS			
Food, Supplies, Grooming			
MISCELLANEOUS			
Copies, Office Supplies			
Gifts, Cards			
Lottery			
Tithe, Donations			
TOTAL			
ATM WITHDRAWALS			
DEBIT CASH WITHDRAWALS			

THUR	FRI	SAT	SUN	TOTAL

MONTHLY MONEY JOURNAL

(Notes/Reflections/Insights/Progress)

Use these pages to jot down your thoughts and experiences with money as you go through the month.

Did you notice any spending patterns?

....

....

....

Are there consistent thoughts or feelings you noticed when spending at certain times or on specific items?

....

....

....

Were you surprised at how much you spent in certain areas?

....

....

....

Were you delighted to see how long your money lasted or how little you spent in some areas?

....

....

....

Have you come up with changes you want to make?

....

....

....

Other comments:

....

....

....

....

SPLURGE DIARY

Use these pages for those times when your spending is totally unplanned and way over budget. By recording your feelings and circumstances about a particular spending event you can begin to get in touch with some deeper reasons for spending.

Date	What I bought or spent money on	Amount	Cash	Charge
....	....	....	....	....
....	....	....	....	....
....	....	....	....	....
....	....	....	....	....

What happened right before the spending?

....

....

....

How was I feeling at that time?

....

....

....

How did I feel during the spending?

....

....

....

How did I feel a few hours later?

....

....

....

Sample feelings: *depressed, angry, excited, empty, lonely, guilty, shamed, remorseful, anxious, frantic, bored, nervous, powerful, deserving, noticed, confused, worried, fearful, hopeless, accepted, resentful, overwhelmed, tired, needy, disappointed*

How did I feel the next day and/or a week later?

....

....

....

What did I do as a result of that spending?

....

....

....

What did I learn about myself (my habits, feelings, patterns, thoughts)?

....

....

....

What unmet needs am I possibly trying to meet through my spending?

....

....

....

Who or what do these feelings remind me of from my past?

....

....

....

Next time, what can I do to replace the spending urge?
(See Alternative Activities List.)

....

....

....

Changes I've made since that spending:

....

....

....

Notes/Reflections/Insights:

VICTORY DIARY

Use these pages for those times when you *successfully did not give in* to your spending urges. Changing your spending patterns is a very positive and significant event, so acknowledge yourself on these occasions.

Date	What I *almost* bought or spent money on	Amount	Cash	Charge
....	....	....	....	....
....	....	....	....	....
....	....	....	....	....
....	....	....	....	....

What happened right before the spending urge?

....

....

....

How was I feeling at that time?

....

....

....

What did I do to *replace* the spending urge?

....

....

....

How did I feel immediately after deciding *not* to spend the money?

....

....

....

Sample feelings: *powerful, in charge, victorious, calm, relaxed, happy, proud, content, honest, satisfied, hopeful, validated, accepted, delighted, responsible, free*

How did I feel a few hours later?

....

....

....

How did I feel the next day and/or a week later?

....

....

....

What did I learn about myself (my habits, feelings, patterns, beliefs)?

....

....

....

I am proud of myself because:

....

....

....

How did I reward myself (praised myself, read a book, prepared a pleasant meal, took a nap, spent time on crafts or hobbies, took a drive, walked the dog, etc.)?

....

....

....

Notes/Reflections/Insights:

ALTERNATIVE ACTIVITIES LIST

For Replacing Spending Urges

Having the urge to spend, for some people, can be a very powerful feeling, so it is not easy to just *will it away*. When the urge comes up, you might try postponing it by engaging in another activity. I have listed some low-cost, no-cost activity ideas to help you gradually find ways to replace those urges with new, more positive behavior.

Try them out and see what works best for you. Your ideas are probably the most creative, so be sure to add many of your own.

These suggestions are especially effective if you are at the stage where you recognize you have behaviors and feelings associated with spending money. If your spending behavior has become much more serious and feels out of control, please see the Resource Guide in the back of the book for help.

Instead of spending at this particular time, I can . . .

✔ Use the 24-hour technique: *Tell yourself that you can buy this item. You can buy it tomorrow. You are choosing to wait 24 hours.*

- ✔ *Call a supportive friend or sponsor and talk about the events of the day and your feelings*

- ✔ *Take a walk or a drive, bike ride, hike, rollerblade or go to the gym*

- ✔ *Read a good story in a book or magazine*

- ✔ *Spend time on your favorite hobby or craft*

- ✔ *Watch a great movie*

- ✔ *Take in a museum, zoo or the botanical gardens*

- ✔ *Play with your children or your pets*

- ✔ *Have your partner give you a massage*

- ✔ *Take a bath or a nap*

- ✔ *Listen to music*

- ✔ *Meditate*

- ✔ *Now add your own*

My favorite activities to do or new things to try are:

....

....

....

....

....

JULY

Questions to ponder when reviewing
finances or right before spending . . .

Is this item a need or a want?

Will it add value to my life now?

How long will I savor the pleasure of this purchase?

---

*"By modifying my behaviors and attitudes, I saved $5,000
this year and am still able to participate as part of the team
(work). The satisfying part is that I always know I can spend
something if I want to."*

In the beginning, it was hard to make ends meet. I never
seemed to have enough money left. I had extra payment fees
for overnight delivery services to meet my obligations and felt
I was rushing around to pay bills. I didn't have extra money
to help me make more money in my business as a REALTOR®.

Then I found the *Common Cent$* book (now *The Budget
Kit*) and hired my bookkeeper/accountant, Roslyn, who
worked with me in outlining upcoming expenses, entered all
my daily spending records and paid all my bills.

I changed to using only cash and put the credit cards aside. Now in the beginning of the week, I lay out the budget, what my needs are for gas, known meals and any other expenses—business or otherwise—and then take the cash. Usually $50 to $100 a week covers the usual expenses. If I don't have cash for something I want then I don't spend the money.

I've been in debt and finally realized if I don't do something, no one else will do it for me. I don't use a checking account or ATM card, and the credit cards are not there for me to use except for an emergency or business expense that I pay off each month. When I'm out shopping and see something I want, I wait until the following day and often decide against the purchase. My accountant will make me think about the spending, too, reminding me that I already have these things and encouraging me when the items are important and of value to me and my business.

I have an A1 credit rating. I got into a new habit, set new goals, established a budget that I follow without variance. The bills are paid by Roslyn when they arrive. By the end of December, all the bills are paid, itemized in her computer and ready for the tax accountant, so I no longer have to worry or agonize over the taxes.

The point of doing this was to set financial goals for the first time in my life. Last year, I cleared up a past tax bill. This year, I cleared up all debt and have the savings to buy my laptop computer, printer, modem and more. Next year, I'm planning a well-deserved two-week cruise or some other special vacation.

I have learned to be clear and disciplined about what I want and need. I know where I have been, and it has helped to plan where I am going.

Lynden Galloway, Santa Fe, N.M.
REALTOR®, Remax/One

JULY   WEEK OF: _____

HOME	MON	TUES	WED
Groceries			
Meals Out			
Snacks, Beverages, Liquor			
Supplies, Furnishings			
TRANSPORTATION			
Gas, Public Transportation			
Vehicle Expense			
PERSONAL CARE			
Clothing, Accessories			
Laundry, Shoe Care			
Hair Care, Toiletries			
Nails, Massage			
ENTERTAINMENT			
Movies, Videos			
CDs, Books			
Hobbies, Sports, Gym			
HEALTH CARE			
Prescriptions, Supplements			
Doctors, Dentists			
CHILDREN			
Child Care, Sitter			
Allowance, School Expense			
PETS			
Food, Supplies, Grooming			
MISCELLANEOUS			
Copies, Office Supplies			
Gifts, Cards			
Lottery			
Tithe, Donations			
TOTAL			
ATM WITHDRAWALS			
DEBIT CASH WITHDRAWALS			

THUR	FRI	SAT	SUN	TOTAL

JULY WEEK OF: _____

HOME	MON	TUES	WED
Groceries			
Meals Out			
Snacks, Beverages, Liquor			
Supplies, Furnishings			
TRANSPORTATION			
Gas, Public Transportation			
Vehicle Expense			
PERSONAL CARE			
Clothing, Accessories			
Laundry, Shoe Care			
Hair Care, Toiletries			
Nails, Massage			
ENTERTAINMENT			
Movies, Videos			
CDs, Books			
Hobbies, Sports, Gym			
HEALTH CARE			
Prescriptions, Supplements			
Doctors, Dentists			
CHILDREN			
Child Care, Sitter			
Allowance, School Expense			
PETS			
Food, Supplies, Grooming			
MISCELLANEOUS			
Copies, Office Supplies			
Gifts, Cards			
Lottery			
Tithe, Donations			
TOTAL			
ATM WITHDRAWALS			
DEBIT CASH WITHDRAWALS			

THUR	FRI	SAT	SUN	TOTAL

JULY WEEK OF: _____

HOME	MON	TUES	WED
Groceries			
Meals Out			
Snacks, Beverages, Liquor			
Supplies, Furnishings			
TRANSPORTATION			
Gas, Public Transportation			
Vehicle Expense			
PERSONAL CARE			
Clothing, Accessories			
Laundry, Shoe Care			
Hair Care, Toiletries			
Nails, Massage			
ENTERTAINMENT			
Movies, Videos			
CDs, Books			
Hobbies, Sports, Gym			
HEALTH CARE			
Prescriptions, Supplements			
Doctors, Dentists			
CHILDREN			
Child Care, Sitter			
Allowance, School Expense			
PETS			
Food, Supplies, Grooming			
MISCELLANEOUS			
Copies, Office Supplies			
Gifts, Cards			
Lottery			
Tithe, Donations			
TOTAL			
ATM WITHDRAWALS			
DEBIT CASH WITHDRAWALS			

THUR	FRI	SAT	SUN	TOTAL

JULY WEEK OF: _____

HOME	MON	TUES	WED
Groceries			
Meals Out			
Snacks, Beverages, Liquor			
Supplies, Furnishings			
TRANSPORTATION			
Gas, Public Transportation			
Vehicle Expense			
PERSONAL CARE			
Clothing, Accessories			
Laundry, Shoe Care			
Hair Care, Toiletries			
Nails, Massage			
ENTERTAINMENT			
Movies, Videos			
CDs, Books			
Hobbies, Sports, Gym			
HEALTH CARE			
Prescriptions, Supplements			
Doctors, Dentists			
CHILDREN			
Child Care, Sitter			
Allowance, School Expense			
PETS			
Food, Supplies, Grooming			
MISCELLANEOUS			
Copies, Office Supplies			
Gifts, Cards			
Lottery			
Tithe, Donations			
TOTAL			
ATM WITHDRAWALS			
DEBIT CASH WITHDRAWALS			

THUR	FRI	SAT	SUN	TOTAL

JULY WEEK OF: _____

HOME	MON	TUES	WED
Groceries			
Meals Out			
Snacks, Beverages, Liquor			
Supplies, Furnishings			
TRANSPORTATION			
Gas, Public Transportation			
Vehicle Expense			
PERSONAL CARE			
Clothing, Accessories			
Laundry, Shoe Care			
Hair Care, Toiletries			
Nails, Massage			
ENTERTAINMENT			
Movies, Videos			
CDs, Books			
Hobbies, Sports, Gym			
HEALTH CARE			
Prescriptions, Supplements			
Doctors, Dentists			
CHILDREN			
Child Care, Sitter			
Allowance, School Expense			
PETS			
Food, Supplies, Grooming			
MISCELLANEOUS			
Copies, Office Supplies			
Gifts, Cards			
Lottery			
Tithe, Donations			
TOTAL			
ATM WITHDRAWALS			
DEBIT CASH WITHDRAWALS			

THUR	FRI	SAT	SUN	TOTAL

MONTHLY MONEY JOURNAL

(Notes/Reflections/Insights/Progress)

Use these pages to jot down your thoughts and experiences with money as you go through the month.

Did you notice any spending patterns?

....

....

....

Are there consistent thoughts or feelings you noticed when spending at certain times or on specific items?

....

....

....

Were you surprised at how much you spent in certain areas?

....

....

....

Were you delighted to see how long your money lasted or how little you spent in some areas?

....

....

....

Have you come up with changes you want to make?

....

....

....

Other comments:

....

....

....

....

SPLURGE DIARY

Use these pages for those times when your spending is totally unplanned and way over budget. By recording your feelings and circumstances about a particular spending event you can begin to get in touch with some deeper reasons for spending.

Date	What I bought or spent money on	Amount	Cash	Charge
....	....	....	....	....
....	....	....	....	....
....	....	....	....	....
....	....	....	....	....

What happened right before the spending?

....

....

....

How was I feeling at that time?

....

....

....

How did I feel during the spending?

....

....

....

How did I feel a few hours later?

....

....

....

Sample feelings: *depressed, angry, excited, empty, lonely, guilty, shamed, remorseful, anxious, frantic, bored, nervous, powerful, deserving, noticed, confused, worried, fearful, hopeless, accepted, resentful, overwhelmed, tired, needy, disappointed*

How did I feel the next day and/or a week later?

....

....

....

What did I do as a result of that spending?

....

....

....

What did I learn about myself (my habits, feelings, patterns, thoughts)?

....

....

....

What unmet needs am I possibly trying to meet through my spending?

....

....

....

Who or what do these feelings remind me of from my past?

....

....

....

Next time, what can I do to replace the spending urge?
(See Alternative Activities List.)

....

....

....

Changes I've made since that spending:

....

....

....

Notes/Reflections/Insights:

VICTORY DIARY

Use these pages for those times when you *successfully did not give in* to your spending urges. Changing your spending patterns is a very positive and significant event, so acknowledge yourself on these occasions.

Date	What I *almost* bought or spent money on	Amount	Cash	Charge
....	....	....	....	....
....	....	....	....	....
....	....	....	....	....
....	....	....	....	....

What happened right before the spending urge?

....

....

....

How was I feeling at that time?

....

....

....

What did I do to *replace* the spending urge?

....

....

....

How did I feel immediately after deciding *not* to spend the money?

....

....

....

Sample feelings: *powerful, in charge, victorious, calm, relaxed, happy, proud, content, honest, satisfied, hopeful, validated, accepted, delighted, responsible, free*

How did I feel a few hours later?

....

....

....

How did I feel the next day and/or a week later?

....

....

....

What did I learn about myself (my habits, feelings, patterns, beliefs)?

....

....

....

I am proud of myself because:

....

....

....

How did I reward myself (praised myself, read a book, prepared a pleasant meal, took a nap, spent time on crafts or hobbies, took a drive, walked the dog, etc.)?

....

....

....

Notes/Reflections/Insights:

ALTERNATIVE ACTIVITIES LIST

For Replacing Spending Urges

Having the urge to spend, for some people, can be a very powerful feeling, so it is not easy to just *will it away*. When the urge comes up, you might try postponing it by engaging in another activity. I have listed some low-cost, no-cost activity ideas to help you gradually find ways to replace those urges with new, more positive behavior.

Try them out and see what works best for you. Your ideas are probably the most creative, so be sure to add many of your own.

These suggestions are especially effective if you are at the stage where you recognize you have behaviors and feelings associated with spending money. If your spending behavior has become much more serious and feels out of control, please see the Resource Guide in the back of the book for help.

Instead of spending at this particular time, I can . . .

✔ *Use the 24-hour technique: Tell yourself that you can buy this item. You can buy it tomorrow. You are choosing to wait 24 hours.*

- ✔ *Call a supportive friend or sponsor and talk about the events of the day and your feelings*

- ✔ *Take a walk or a drive, bike ride, hike, rollerblade or go to the gym*

- ✔ *Read a good story in a book or magazine*

- ✔ *Spend time on your favorite hobby or craft*

- ✔ *Watch a great movie*

- ✔ *Take in a museum, zoo or the botanical gardens*

- ✔ *Play with your children or your pets*

- ✔ *Have your partner give you a massage*

- ✔ *Take a bath or a nap*

- ✔ *Listen to music*

- ✔ *Meditate*

- ✔ *Now add your own*

My favorite activities to do or new things to try are:

....

....

....

....

....

AUGUST

Questions to ponder when reviewing
finances or right before spending . . .

**If I put off spending until tomorrow for what I
want today, how do I usually feel or react?**

**Will the pleasure of this purchase today outweigh the
stress of a future shortage of money in another area?**

**Can I borrow or rent this item I want to purchase
from someone or someplace instead of buying it?**

---

*"Keeping records helps me to see where I have spent
too much money. It also helps me save money with my
accountant, who tells me I've got all the records I need for
my taxes in this book."*

I keep track of all of our spending on the big spending areas,
especially eating out, tips and gas. If possible, I try to log expenses each night so I make a habit of collecting lots of receipts during the day. I try never to go longer than three to
four days without logging my expenses.

With all these records, I can clearly see where the money has gone and I can forecast how much extra money needs to come in. I can see it on paper. When I show my husband, the information really hits home, more so than when I'm just telling him about our upcoming expenses. I am able to anticipate well in advance what extra money my husband needs to earn at his part-time job for upcoming expenses like tuition, sports events or vacations. Having all of our records also helps when planning how many months it will take to pay off certain debts.

I would be lost without the ability to project. My husband knows we would be in a big jam if I didn't handle finances the way I do. We don't have a lot of extra money, so this control helps us to manage our money most effectively.

We realize one of our high spending areas is eating out and have decided this is just a spending area we accept due to our lifestyle. Our kids are involved in many sports and my husband has an erratic schedule, so it's easier to just stop and grab something to eat on the run. Our meals-out expense is $400 a month. Since I go to all the children's games, by the time we walk in the door there is no time to spend in the kitchen preparing meals. That's probably why our groceries for the four of us run only $300 a month. My priority is to be out there with my kids at their games. We don't drink, smoke, go out or engage in other expensive activities, so we feel comfortable with this expense.

We are able to stay on top of everything and feel financially stable. A few years ago, we were able to buy a house because of our good credit. The only reason we maintain this good credit is because we know what expenses and events are coming up, and we keep track of all our expenses.

Georgie and Troy Thurmond, Orange Park, Fla.
Housewife/Operating Room Nurse, Age 40
Two Children, Ages 14 and 11

AUGUST WEEK OF: _____

HOME	MON	TUES	WED
Groceries			
Meals Out			
Snacks, Beverages, Liquor			
Supplies, Furnishings			
TRANSPORTATION			
Gas, Public Transportation			
Vehicle Expense			
PERSONAL CARE			
Clothing, Accessories			
Laundry, Shoe Care			
Hair Care, Toiletries			
Nails, Massage			
ENTERTAINMENT			
Movies, Videos			
CDs, Books			
Hobbies, Sports, Gym			
HEALTH CARE			
Prescriptions, Supplements			
Doctors, Dentists			
CHILDREN			
Child Care, Sitter			
Allowance, School Expense			
PETS			
Food, Supplies, Grooming			
MISCELLANEOUS			
Copies, Office Supplies			
Gifts, Cards			
Lottery			
Tithe, Donations			
TOTAL			
ATM WITHDRAWALS			
DEBIT CASH WITHDRAWALS			

THUR	FRI	SAT	SUN	TOTAL

AUGUST WEEK OF: _____

HOME	MON	TUES	WED
Groceries			
Meals Out			
Snacks, Beverages, Liquor			
Supplies, Furnishings			
TRANSPORTATION			
Gas, Public Transportation			
Vehicle Expense			
PERSONAL CARE			
Clothing, Accessories			
Laundry, Shoe Care			
Hair Care, Toiletries			
Nails, Massage			
ENTERTAINMENT			
Movies, Videos			
CDs, Books			
Hobbies, Sports, Gym			
HEALTH CARE			
Prescriptions, Supplements			
Doctors, Dentists			
CHILDREN			
Child Care, Sitter			
Allowance, School Expense			
PETS			
Food, Supplies, Grooming			
MISCELLANEOUS			
Copies, Office Supplies			
Gifts, Cards			
Lottery			
Tithe, Donations			
TOTAL			
ATM WITHDRAWALS			
DEBIT CASH WITHDRAWALS			

THUR	FRI	SAT	SUN	TOTAL

AUGUST WEEK OF: _____

HOME	MON	TUES	WED
Groceries			
Meals Out			
Snacks, Beverages, Liquor			
Supplies, Furnishings			
TRANSPORTATION			
Gas, Public Transportation			
Vehicle Expense			
PERSONAL CARE			
Clothing, Accessories			
Laundry, Shoe Care			
Hair Care, Toiletries			
Nails, Massage			
ENTERTAINMENT			
Movies, Videos			
CDs, Books			
Hobbies, Sports, Gym			
HEALTH CARE			
Prescriptions, Supplements			
Doctors, Dentists			
CHILDREN			
Child Care, Sitter			
Allowance, School Expense			
PETS			
Food, Supplies, Grooming			
MISCELLANEOUS			
Copies, Office Supplies			
Gifts, Cards			
Lottery			
Tithe, Donations			
TOTAL			
ATM WITHDRAWALS			
DEBIT CASH WITHDRAWALS			

THUR	FRI	SAT	SUN	TOTAL

AUGUST WEEK OF: _____

HOME	MON	TUES	WED
Groceries			
Meals Out			
Snacks, Beverages, Liquor			
Supplies, Furnishings			
TRANSPORTATION			
Gas, Public Transportation			
Vehicle Expense			
PERSONAL CARE			
Clothing, Accessories			
Laundry, Shoe Care			
Hair Care, Toiletries			
Nails, Massage			
ENTERTAINMENT			
Movies, Videos			
CDs, Books			
Hobbies, Sports, Gym			
HEALTH CARE			
Prescriptions, Supplements			
Doctors, Dentists			
CHILDREN			
Child Care, Sitter			
Allowance, School Expense			
PETS			
Food, Supplies, Grooming			
MISCELLANEOUS			
Copies, Office Supplies			
Gifts, Cards			
Lottery			
Tithe, Donations			
TOTAL			
ATM WITHDRAWALS			
DEBIT CASH WITHDRAWALS			

THUR	FRI	SAT	SUN	TOTAL

AUGUST WEEK OF: _____

HOME	MON	TUES	WED
Groceries			
Meals Out			
Snacks, Beverages, Liquor			
Supplies, Furnishings			
TRANSPORTATION			
Gas, Public Transportation			
Vehicle Expense			
PERSONAL CARE			
Clothing, Accessories			
Laundry, Shoe Care			
Hair Care, Toiletries			
Nails, Massage			
ENTERTAINMENT			
Movies, Videos			
CDs, Books			
Hobbies, Sports, Gym			
HEALTH CARE			
Prescriptions, Supplements			
Doctors, Dentists			
CHILDREN			
Child Care, Sitter			
Allowance, School Expense			
PETS			
Food, Supplies, Grooming			
MISCELLANEOUS			
Copies, Office Supplies			
Gifts, Cards			
Lottery			
Tithe, Donations			
TOTAL			
ATM WITHDRAWALS			
DEBIT CASH WITHDRAWALS			

THUR	FRI	SAT	SUN	TOTAL

MONTHLY MONEY JOURNAL

(Notes/Reflections/Insights/Progress)

Use these pages to jot down your thoughts and experiences with money as you go through the month.

Did you notice any spending patterns?

....

....

....

Are there consistent thoughts or feelings you noticed when spending at certain times or on specific items?

....

....

....

Were you surprised at how much you spent in certain areas?

....

....

....

Were you delighted to see how long your money lasted or how little you spent in some areas?

....

....

....

Have you come up with changes you want to make?

....

....

....

Other comments:

....

....

....

....

SPLURGE DIARY

Use these pages for those times when your spending is totally unplanned and way over budget. By recording your feelings and circumstances about a particular spending event you can begin to get in touch with some deeper reasons for spending.

Date	What I bought or spent money on	Amount	Cash	Charge
....	....	....	....	....
....	....	....	....	....
....	....	....	....	....
....	....	....	....	....

What happened right before the spending?

....

....

....

How was I feeling at that time?

....

....

....

How did I feel during the spending?

....

....

....

How did I feel a few hours later?

....

....

....

Sample feelings: *depressed, angry, excited, empty, lonely, guilty, shamed, remorseful, anxious, frantic, bored, nervous, powerful, deserving, noticed, confused, worried, fearful, hopeless, accepted, resentful, overwhelmed, tired, needy, disappointed*

How did I feel the next day and/or a week later?

....

....

....

What did I do as a result of that spending?

....

....

....

What did I learn about myself (my habits, feelings, patterns, thoughts)?

....

....

....

What unmet needs am I possibly trying to meet through my spending?

....

....

....

Who or what do these feelings remind me of from my past?

....

....

....

Next time, what can I do to replace the spending urge?
(See Alternative Activities List.)

....

....

....

Changes I've made since that spending:

....

....

....

Notes/Reflections/Insights:

VICTORY DIARY

Use these pages for those times when you *successfully did not give in* to your spending urges. Changing your spending patterns is a very positive and significant event, so acknowledge yourself on these occasions.

Date	What I *almost* bought or spent money on	Amount	Cash	Charge
....	....	....	....	....
....	....	....	....	....
....	....	....	....	....
....	....	....	....	....

What happened right before the spending urge?

....

....

....

How was I feeling at that time?

....

....

....

What did I do to *replace* the spending urge?

....

....

....

How did I feel immediately after deciding *not* to spend the money?

....

....

....

Sample feelings: *powerful, in charge, victorious, calm, relaxed, happy, proud, content, honest, satisfied, hopeful, validated, accepted, delighted, responsible, free*

How did I feel a few hours later?

....

....

....

How did I feel the next day and/or a week later?

....

....

....

What did I learn about myself (my habits, feelings, patterns, beliefs)?

....

....

....

I am proud of myself because:

....

....

....

How did I reward myself (praised myself, read a book, prepared a pleasant meal, took a nap, spent time on crafts or hobbies, took a drive, walked the dog, etc.)?

....

....

....

Notes/Reflections/Insights:

ALTERNATIVE ACTIVITIES LIST

For Replacing Spending Urges

Having the urge to spend, for some people, can be a very powerful feeling, so it is not easy to just *will it away*. When the urge comes up, you might try postponing it by engaging in another activity. I have listed some low-cost, no-cost activity ideas to help you gradually find ways to replace those urges with new, more positive behavior.

Try them out and see what works best for you. Your ideas are probably the most creative, so be sure to add many of your own.

These suggestions are especially effective if you are at the stage where you recognize you have behaviors and feelings associated with spending money. If your spending behavior has become much more serious and feels out of control, please see the Resource Guide in the back of the book for help.

Instead of spending at this particular time, I can ...

- ✔ *Use the 24-hour technique: Tell yourself that you can buy this item. You can buy it tomorrow. You are choosing to wait 24 hours.*

- ✔ Call a supportive friend or sponsor and talk about the events of the day and your feelings

- ✔ Take a walk or a drive, bike ride, hike, rollerblade or go to the gym

- ✔ Read a good story in a book or magazine

- ✔ Spend time on your favorite hobby or craft

- ✔ Watch a great movie

- ✔ Take in a museum, zoo or the botanical gardens

- ✔ Play with your children or your pets

- ✔ Have your partner give you a massage

- ✔ Take a bath or a nap

- ✔ Listen to music

- ✔ Meditate

- ✔ Now add your own

My favorite activities to do or new things to try are:

....

....

....

....

....

SEPTEMBER

Questions to ponder when reviewing
finances or right before spending . . .

**Are there any end-of-summer sales that will
save me money on budgeted items?**

**If I buy a season ticket to my favorite theater,
symphony or athletic game, do I attend enough
of the events so I am still saving money?**

**Do I sometimes buy things I don't need with money
I don't have to impress people I don't even
like or to fill some emptiness?**

---

*"We have put aside three months of salary for emergency
money plus a general savings account for all upcoming expenses. We managed to save, even during three maternity leaves
and a period of part-time work while completing an MBA."*

When Mark and I got married in 1982, we didn't know how
to make a budget. Now we sit down every December and
work out the budget for the next year. We map out our income for the year and anticipate month by month how much

we will spend in each expense category. After that, we know how much extra we will have each month.

We put money aside each year and project our income and expenses, so that we know what we can purchase the following year and plan our yearly goals. One year our goal was new living room furniture, another year a vacation. This year we added 1,100 square feet to the house. When I took a six-month maternity leave, we planned the monthly expenses for the year and put money aside ahead of time to cover extra car and house payments.

Having a specific budgeted amount each month works for us. In July and August, we budget $500 per month to cover clothes for the children and both parents. Then $200 in April for vacation clothes and bathing suits for the children as we make our annual Florida visit. I plan the meals carefully and buy groceries every two weeks and do not go to the store any other time except for milk and bread. As a mother who works outside the home, my time is too precious. Our total grocery bill is usually just under $500 a month for the five of us.

We use a "checks and balance" system: I write the checks, and my husband balances the checkbook. This way we are both aware of our current financial status. If we have an unusual month, we will both sit down again and talk about what happened and make decisions to adjust the budget. If some unusual expense comes up and we go over in some area, then we pull from savings. There's a security knowing we have the savings and the means to cover expenses.

This budgeting system works very well for us. We have really never had debts or problems with our finances.

Lisa and Mark Zetts, Canfield, Ohio
Elementary Teacher/College Professor,
    Ages 36 and 37
Three Children, Ages 7, 5 and 2

SEPTEMBER   WEEK OF: _____

HOME	MON	TUES	WED
Groceries			
Meals Out			
Snacks, Beverages, Liquor			
Supplies, Furnishings			
TRANSPORTATION			
Gas, Public Transportation			
Vehicle Expense			
PERSONAL CARE			
Clothing, Accessories			
Laundry, Shoe Care			
Hair Care, Toiletries			
Nails, Massage			
ENTERTAINMENT			
Movies, Videos			
CDs, Books			
Hobbies, Sports, Gym			
HEALTH CARE			
Prescriptions, Supplements			
Doctors, Dentists			
CHILDREN			
Child Care, Sitter			
Allowance, School Expense			
PETS			
Food, Supplies, Grooming			
MISCELLANEOUS			
Copies, Office Supplies			
Gifts, Cards			
Lottery			
Tithe, Donations			
TOTAL			
ATM WITHDRAWALS			
DEBIT CASH WITHDRAWALS			

THUR	FRI	SAT	SUN	TOTAL

SEPTEMBER WEEK OF: _____

HOME	MON	TUES	WED
Groceries			
Meals Out			
Snacks, Beverages, Liquor			
Supplies, Furnishings			
TRANSPORTATION			
Gas, Public Transportation			
Vehicle Expense			
PERSONAL CARE			
Clothing, Accessories			
Laundry, Shoe Care			
Hair Care, Toiletries			
Nails, Massage			
ENTERTAINMENT			
Movies, Videos			
CDs, Books			
Hobbies, Sports, Gym			
HEALTH CARE			
Prescriptions, Supplements			
Doctors, Dentists			
CHILDREN			
Child Care, Sitter			
Allowance, School Expense			
PETS			
Food, Supplies, Grooming			
MISCELLANEOUS			
Copies, Office Supplies			
Gifts, Cards			
Lottery			
Tithe, Donations			
TOTAL			
ATM WITHDRAWALS			
DEBIT CASH WITHDRAWALS			

THUR	FRI	SAT	SUN	TOTAL

SEPTEMBER   WEEK OF: _____

HOME	MON	TUES	WED
Groceries			
Meals Out			
Snacks, Beverages, Liquor			
Supplies, Furnishings			
TRANSPORTATION			
Gas, Public Transportation			
Vehicle Expense			
PERSONAL CARE			
Clothing, Accessories			
Laundry, Shoe Care			
Hair Care, Toiletries			
Nails, Massage			
ENTERTAINMENT			
Movies, Videos			
CDs, Books			
Hobbies, Sports, Gym			
HEALTH CARE			
Prescriptions, Supplements			
Doctors, Dentists			
CHILDREN			
Child Care, Sitter			
Allowance, School Expense			
PETS			
Food, Supplies, Grooming			
MISCELLANEOUS			
Copies, Office Supplies			
Gifts, Cards			
Lottery			
Tithe, Donations			
TOTAL			
ATM WITHDRAWALS			
DEBIT CASH WITHDRAWALS			

THUR	FRI	SAT	SUN	TOTAL

SEPTEMBER WEEK OF: _____

HOME	MON	TUES	WED
Groceries			
Meals Out			
Snacks, Beverages, Liquor			
Supplies, Furnishings			
TRANSPORTATION			
Gas, Public Transportation			
Vehicle Expense			
PERSONAL CARE			
Clothing, Accessories			
Laundry, Shoe Care			
Hair Care, Toiletries			
Nails, Massage			
ENTERTAINMENT			
Movies, Videos			
CDs, Books			
Hobbies, Sports, Gym			
HEALTH CARE			
Prescriptions, Supplements			
Doctors, Dentists			
CHILDREN			
Child Care, Sitter			
Allowance, School Expense			
PETS			
Food, Supplies, Grooming			
MISCELLANEOUS			
Copies, Office Supplies			
Gifts, Cards			
Lottery			
Tithe, Donations			
TOTAL			
ATM WITHDRAWALS			
DEBIT CASH WITHDRAWALS			

THUR	FRI	SAT	SUN	TOTAL

SEPTEMBER WEEK OF: _____

HOME	MON	TUES	WED
Groceries			
Meals Out			
Snacks, Beverages, Liquor			
Supplies, Furnishings			
TRANSPORTATION			
Gas, Public Transportation			
Vehicle Expense			
PERSONAL CARE			
Clothing, Accessories			
Laundry, Shoe Care			
Hair Care, Toiletries			
Nails, Massage			
ENTERTAINMENT			
Movies, Videos			
CDs, Books			
Hobbies, Sports, Gym			
HEALTH CARE			
Prescriptions, Supplements			
Doctors, Dentists			
CHILDREN			
Child Care, Sitter			
Allowance, School Expense			
PETS			
Food, Supplies, Grooming			
MISCELLANEOUS			
Copies, Office Supplies			
Gifts, Cards			
Lottery			
Tithe, Donations			
TOTAL			
ATM WITHDRAWALS			
DEBIT CASH WITHDRAWALS			

THUR	FRI	SAT	SUN	TOTAL

MONTHLY MONEY JOURNAL

(Notes/Reflections/Insights/Progress)

Use these pages to jot down your thoughts and experiences with money as you go through the month.

Did you notice any spending patterns?

....

....

....

Are there consistent thoughts or feelings you noticed when spending at certain times or on specific items?

....

....

....

Were you surprised at how much you spent in certain areas?

....

....

....

Were you delighted to see how long your money lasted or
how little you spent in some areas?

....

....

....

Have you come up with changes you want to make?

....

....

....

Other comments:

....

....

....

....

SPLURGE DIARY

Use these pages for those times when your spending is totally unplanned and way over budget. By recording your feelings and circumstances about a particular spending event you can begin to get in touch with some deeper reasons for spending.

Date	What I bought or spent money on	Amount	Cash	Charge
....	....	....	....	....
....	....	....	....	....
....	....	....	....	....
....	....	....	....	....

What happened right before the spending?

....

....

....

How was I feeling at that time?

....

....

....

How did I feel during the spending?

....

....

....

How did I feel a few hours later?

....

....

....

Sample feelings: *depressed, angry, excited, empty, lonely, guilty, shamed, remorseful, anxious, frantic, bored, nervous, powerful, deserving, noticed, confused, worried, fearful, hopeless, accepted, resentful, overwhelmed, tired, needy, disappointed*

How did I feel the next day and/or a week later?

....

....

....

What did I do as a result of that spending?

....

....

....

What did I learn about myself (my habits, feelings, patterns, thoughts)?

....

....

....

What unmet needs am I possibly trying to meet through my spending?

....

....

....

Who or what do these feelings remind me of from my past?

....

....

....

Next time, what can I do to replace the spending urge?
(See Alternative Activities List.)

....

....

....

Changes I've made since that spending:

....

....

....

Notes/Reflections/Insights:

VICTORY DIARY

Use these pages for those times when you *successfully did not give in* to your spending urges. Changing your spending patterns is a very positive and significant event, so acknowledge yourself on these occasions.

Date	What I *almost* bought or spent money on	Amount	Cash	Charge
....	....	....	....	....
....	....	....	....	....
....	....	....	....	....
....	....	....	....	....

What happened right before the spending urge?

....

....

....

How was I feeling at that time?

....

....

....

What did I do to *replace* the spending urge?

....

....

....

How did I feel immediately after deciding *not* to spend the money?

....

....

....

Sample feelings: *powerful, in charge, victorious, calm, relaxed, happy, proud, content, honest, satisfied, hopeful, validated, accepted, delighted, responsible, free*

How did I feel a few hours later?

....

....

....

How did I feel the next day and/or a week later?

....

....

....

What did I learn about myself (my habits, feelings, patterns, beliefs)?

....

....

....

I am proud of myself because:

....

....

....

How did I reward myself (praised myself, read a book, prepared a pleasant meal, took a nap, spent time on crafts or hobbies, took a drive, walked the dog, etc.)?

....

....

....

Notes/Reflections/Insights:

ALTERNATIVE ACTIVITIES LIST

For Replacing Spending Urges

Having the urge to spend, for some people, can be a very powerful feeling, so it is not easy to just *will it away*. When the urge comes up, you might try postponing it by engaging in another activity. I have listed some low-cost, no-cost activity ideas to help you gradually find ways to replace those urges with new, more positive behavior.

Try them out and see what works best for you. Your ideas are probably the most creative, so be sure to add many of your own.

These suggestions are especially effective if you are at the stage where you recognize you have behaviors and feelings associated with spending money. If your spending behavior has become much more serious and feels out of control, please see the Resource Guide in the back of the book for help.

Instead of spending at this particular time, I can . . .

✔ *Use the 24-hour technique: Tell yourself that you can buy this item. You can buy it tomorrow. You are choosing to wait 24 hours.*

- ✔ *Call a supportive friend or sponsor and talk about the events of the day and your feelings*

- ✔ *Take a walk or a drive, bike ride, hike, rollerblade or go to the gym*

- ✔ *Read a good story in a book or magazine*

- ✔ *Spend time on your favorite hobby or craft*

- ✔ *Watch a great movie*

- ✔ *Take in a museum, zoo or the botanical gardens*

- ✔ *Play with your children or your pets*

- ✔ *Have your partner give you a massage*

- ✔ *Take a bath or a nap*

- ✔ *Listen to music*

- ✔ *Meditate*

- ✔ *Now add your own*

My favorite activities to do or new things to try are:

....

....

....

....

....

OCTOBER

Questions to ponder when reviewing
finances or right before spending . . .

**Do I need more information (read more literature,
talk to other owners or better business bureaus)
before I make this purchase?**

**How would my life change or be different now
and/or six months from now if I did or did not
spend this money on a particular expense?**

**Will I have a sense of more balance or harmony
in my life after spending this money?**

---

*"As we combine our income and expenses, we'll know
exactly how much money we can spend on the wedding and
honeymoon and still meet all our individual and joint goals
for the year!"*

Before I found *The Budget Kit,* I was always trying to
"find" money to make ends meet—borrowing from my sav-

ings, running helter-skelter looking for extra cash and spending a lot of time worrying about money.

I've been using *The Budget Kit* to track my expenses for two years now, and my best success story happened when I was laid off at the end of 1994. I decided to start my own company, but knew that I'd have to limit expenses while I built my business.

After spending ten minutes going over my 1994 monthly planning worksheets, I was able to quickly see which variable and occasional expenses I could eliminate or cut back on in 1995. Looking back at my 1994 recorded monthly expenses, I was able to spot other areas where I could painlessly pare expenses. And, I was able to see exactly how much money I had to make each month to meet my expenses and save for unexpected or down-the-road big purchases that I knew I needed to make.

Even though I was no longer receiving a monthly salary, I was able to budget for a new computer, completed a $25,000 renovation on my home, paid off my car three months early and still managed to add extra principal to each month's mortgage payment. All because I knew where I needed to spend my money. I even continued to *invest* money each month!

Now that I'm tying the knot, a budget will play an ever bigger role in my life. As we combine our income and expenses, we'll know exactly how much money we can spend on the wedding and honeymoon and still meet all our individual and joint goals for the year!

Paula E. Langguth, Fairhaven, Md.

OCTOBER WEEK OF: _____

HOME	MON	TUES	WED
Groceries			
Meals Out			
Snacks, Beverages, Liquor			
Supplies, Furnishings			
TRANSPORTATION			
Gas, Public Transportation			
Vehicle Expense			
PERSONAL CARE			
Clothing, Accessories			
Laundry, Shoe Care			
Hair Care, Toiletries			
Nails, Massage			
ENTERTAINMENT			
Movies, Videos			
CDs, Books			
Hobbies, Sports, Gym			
HEALTH CARE			
Prescriptions, Supplements			
Doctors, Dentists			
CHILDREN			
Child Care, Sitter			
Allowance, School Expense			
PETS			
Food, Supplies, Grooming			
MISCELLANEOUS			
Copies, Office Supplies			
Gifts, Cards			
Lottery			
Tithe, Donations			
TOTAL			
ATM WITHDRAWALS			
DEBIT CASH WITHDRAWALS			

THUR	FRI	SAT	SUN	TOTAL

OCTOBER WEEK OF: _____

HOME	MON	TUES	WED
Groceries			
Meals Out			
Snacks, Beverages, Liquor			
Supplies, Furnishings			
TRANSPORTATION			
Gas, Public Transportation			
Vehicle Expense			
PERSONAL CARE			
Clothing, Accessories			
Laundry, Shoe Care			
Hair Care, Toiletries			
Nails, Massage			
ENTERTAINMENT			
Movies, Videos			
CDs, Books			
Hobbies, Sports, Gym			
HEALTH CARE			
Prescriptions, Supplements			
Doctors, Dentists			
CHILDREN			
Child Care, Sitter			
Allowance, School Expense			
PETS			
Food, Supplies, Grooming			
MISCELLANEOUS			
Copies, Office Supplies			
Gifts, Cards			
Lottery			
Tithe, Donations			
TOTAL			
ATM WITHDRAWALS			
DEBIT CASH WITHDRAWALS			

THUR	FRI	SAT	SUN	TOTAL

OCTOBER WEEK OF: _____

HOME	MON	TUES	WED
Groceries			
Meals Out			
Snacks, Beverages, Liquor			
Supplies, Furnishings			
TRANSPORTATION			
Gas, Public Transportation			
Vehicle Expense			
PERSONAL CARE			
Clothing, Accessories			
Laundry, Shoe Care			
Hair Care, Toiletries			
Nails, Massage			
ENTERTAINMENT			
Movies, Videos			
CDs, Books			
Hobbies, Sports, Gym			
HEALTH CARE			
Prescriptions, Supplements			
Doctors, Dentists			
CHILDREN			
Child Care, Sitter			
Allowance, School Expense			
PETS			
Food, Supplies, Grooming			
MISCELLANEOUS			
Copies, Office Supplies			
Gifts, Cards			
Lottery			
Tithe, Donations			
TOTAL			
ATM WITHDRAWALS			
DEBIT CASH WITHDRAWALS			

THUR	FRI	SAT	SUN	TOTAL

OCTOBER WEEK OF: _____

HOME	MON	TUES	WED
Groceries			
Meals Out			
Snacks, Beverages, Liquor			
Supplies, Furnishings			
TRANSPORTATION			
Gas, Public Transportation			
Vehicle Expense			
PERSONAL CARE			
Clothing, Accessories			
Laundry, Shoe Care			
Hair Care, Toiletries			
Nails, Massage			
ENTERTAINMENT			
Movies, Videos			
CDs, Books			
Hobbies, Sports, Gym			
HEALTH CARE			
Prescriptions, Supplements			
Doctors, Dentists			
CHILDREN			
Child Care, Sitter			
Allowance, School Expense			
PETS			
Food, Supplies, Grooming			
MISCELLANEOUS			
Copies, Office Supplies			
Gifts, Cards			
Lottery			
Tithe, Donations			
TOTAL			
ATM WITHDRAWALS			
DEBIT CASH WITHDRAWALS			

THUR	FRI	SAT	SUN	TOTAL

OCTOBER WEEK OF: _____

HOME	MON	TUES	WED
Groceries			
Meals Out			
Snacks, Beverages, Liquor			
Supplies, Furnishings			
TRANSPORTATION			
Gas, Public Transportation			
Vehicle Expense			
PERSONAL CARE			
Clothing, Accessories			
Laundry, Shoe Care			
Hair Care, Toiletries			
Nails, Massage			
ENTERTAINMENT			
Movies, Videos			
CDs, Books			
Hobbies, Sports, Gym			
HEALTH CARE			
Prescriptions, Supplements			
Doctors, Dentists			
CHILDREN			
Child Care, Sitter			
Allowance, School Expense			
PETS			
Food, Supplies, Grooming			
MISCELLANEOUS			
Copies, Office Supplies			
Gifts, Cards			
Lottery			
Tithe, Donations			
TOTAL			
ATM WITHDRAWALS			
DEBIT CASH WITHDRAWALS			

THUR	FRI	SAT	SUN	TOTAL

MONTHLY MONEY JOURNAL

(Notes/Reflections/Insights/Progress)

Use these pages to jot down your thoughts and experiences with money as you go through the month.

Did you notice any spending patterns?

....

....

....

Are there consistent thoughts or feelings you noticed when spending at certain times or on specific items?

....

....

....

Were you surprised at how much you spent in certain areas?

....

....

....

Were you delighted to see how long your money lasted or how little you spent in some areas?

....

....

....

Have you come up with changes you want to make?

....

....

....

Other comments:

....

....

....

....

SPLURGE DIARY

Use these pages for those times when your spending is totally unplanned and way over budget. By recording your feelings and circumstances about a particular spending event you can begin to get in touch with some deeper reasons for spending.

Date	What I bought or spent money on	Amount	Cash	Charge
....	....	....	....	....
....	....	....	....	....
....	....	....	....	....
....	....	....	....	....

What happened right before the spending?

....

....

....

How was I feeling at that time?

....

....

....

How did I feel during the spending?

....

....

....

How did I feel a few hours later?

....

....

....

Sample feelings: *depressed, angry, excited, empty, lonely, guilty, shamed, remorseful, anxious, frantic, bored, nervous, powerful, deserving, noticed, confused, worried, fearful, hopeless, accepted, resentful, overwhelmed, tired, needy, disappointed*

How did I feel the next day and/or a week later?

....

....

....

What did I do as a result of that spending?

....

....

....

What did I learn about myself (my habits, feelings, patterns, thoughts)?

....

....

....

What unmet needs am I possibly trying to meet through my spending?

....

....

....

Who or what do these feelings remind me of from my past?

....

....

....

Next time, what can I do to replace the spending urge?
(See Alternative Activities List.)

....

....

....

Changes I've made since that spending:

....

....

....

Notes/Reflections/Insights:

VICTORY DIARY

Use these pages for those times when you *successfully did not give in* to your spending urges. Changing your spending patterns is a very positive and significant event, so acknowledge yourself on these occasions.

Date	What I *almost* bought or spent money on	Amount	Cash	Charge
....	....	....	....	....
....	....	....	....	....
....	....	....	....	....
....	....	....	....	....

What happened right before the spending urge?

....

....

....

How was I feeling at that time?

....

....

....

What did I do to *replace* the spending urge?

....

....

....

How did I feel immediately after deciding *not* to spend the money?

....

....

....

Sample feelings: *powerful, in charge, victorious, calm, relaxed, happy, proud, content, honest, satisfied, hopeful, validated, accepted, delighted, responsible, free*

How did I feel a few hours later?

....

....

....

How did I feel the next day and/or a week later?

....

....

....

What did I learn about myself (my habits, feelings, patterns, beliefs)?

....

....

....

I am proud of myself because:

....

....

....

How did I reward myself (praised myself, read a book, prepared a pleasant meal, took a nap, spent time on crafts or hobbies, took a drive, walked the dog, etc.)?

....

....

....

Notes/Reflections/Insights:

ALTERNATIVE ACTIVITIES LIST

For Replacing Spending Urges

Having the urge to spend, for some people, can be a very powerful feeling, so it is not easy to just *will it away*. When the urge comes up, you might try postponing it by engaging in another activity. I have listed some low-cost, no-cost activity ideas to help you gradually find ways to replace those urges with new, more positive behavior.

Try them out and see what works best for you. Your ideas are probably the most creative, so be sure to add many of your own.

These suggestions are especially effective if you are at the stage where you recognize you have behaviors and feelings associated with spending money. If your spending behavior has become much more serious and feels out of control, please see the Resource Guide in the back of the book for help.

Instead of spending at this particular time, I can . . .

✔ *Use the 24-hour technique: Tell yourself that you can buy this item. You can buy it tomorrow. You are choosing to wait 24 hours.*

- *Call a supportive friend or sponsor and talk about the events of the day and your feelings*

- *Take a walk or a drive, bike ride, hike, rollerblade or go to the gym*

- *Read a good story in a book or magazine*

- *Spend time on your favorite hobby or craft*

- *Watch a great movie*

- *Take in a museum, zoo or the botanical gardens*

- *Play with your children or your pets*

- *Have your partner give you a massage*

- *Take a bath or a nap*

- *Listen to music*

- *Meditate*

- *Now add your own*

My favorite activities to do or new things to try are:

....

....

....

....

....

NOVEMBER

Questions to ponder when reviewing
finances or right before spending . . .

**How many hours did I have to work to earn
the money for this expense?**

**Is this expense worth the time, the effort and
work it took me to make the money?**

**Is there a difference between how I *think* I spend
my money and how I *actually* spend it?**

---

*"Once I started saving, I was able to save $7,000 for my
wedding over a two-year period."*

Before I started working with a budgeting plan, I was frustrated because I had no system for saving money or paying
expenses. Since I started working with *The Budget Kit,* I sit
down on a regular basis and review my budget.

As I plan the next month's budget, I write down all my
regular bills and figure out other likely expenses, so I know
how much money I will need. For savings, I include an

amount for my trip abroad fund and an amount for my general savings account. I always make sure I am saving money. For example, instead of planning to buy a skirt, I put more money into my trip fund (which adds up to about $1,500 a year). If I really want to buy a skirt, however, I adjust my budget so that I can buy the skirt and still save for my trip.

When I started using a system, I actually became aware of the *cost* of each type of expenditure. I was surprised to realize that I could build a monthly plan to pay for everything from gasoline to an electric bill. Now I save ahead for my bills. I also keep records of my credit card charges, so I know how much to have on hand to pay off the bill each month.

Having a plan also allows me to set up a splurge or "mad money" fund of $200 each pay period. This is my cash for magazines, books, bargains, small meals, clothes and the like. I hate going to ATM machines, so I withdraw this cash at one time, and it carries me through until the next paycheck and gives me a much better sense of financial control.

One thing I know about myself is that if I'm only paying bills and haven't purchased something for myself, I develop an incredible urge to spend. My mad money comes in handy at this time, since some $20 or $30 item like a candle, cookbook or hair product usually satisfies that urge.

Another thing I know about myself is the importance of savings. If the money is in checking, I just spend it. If I put money into savings, it becomes sacrosanct, and I will not touch it. Two years before getting married, I started saving and managed to save $7,000 for the wedding. It was very encouraging to see money in savings and know that money was available for the major wedding expenses. I know I never could have done this well without a plan.

Heather Fonseca, Los Angeles, Calif.
Designer, Age 26

NOVEMBER WEEK OF: _____

HOME	MON	TUES	WED
Groceries			
Meals Out			
Snacks, Beverages, Liquor			
Supplies, Furnishings			
TRANSPORTATION			
Gas, Public Transportation			
Vehicle Expense			
PERSONAL CARE			
Clothing, Accessories			
Laundry, Shoe Care			
Hair Care, Toiletries			
Nails, Massage			
ENTERTAINMENT			
Movies, Videos			
CDs, Books			
Hobbies, Sports, Gym			
HEALTH CARE			
Prescriptions, Supplements			
Doctors, Dentists			
CHILDREN			
Child Care, Sitter			
Allowance, School Expense			
PETS			
Food, Supplies, Grooming			
MISCELLANEOUS			
Copies, Office Supplies			
Gifts, Cards			
Lottery			
Tithe, Donations			
TOTAL			
ATM WITHDRAWALS			
DEBIT CASH WITHDRAWALS			

THUR	FRI	SAT	SUN	TOTAL

NOVEMBER WEEK OF: _____

HOME	MON	TUES	WED
Groceries			
Meals Out			
Snacks, Beverages, Liquor			
Supplies, Furnishings			
TRANSPORTATION			
Gas, Public Transportation			
Vehicle Expense			
PERSONAL CARE			
Clothing, Accessories			
Laundry, Shoe Care			
Hair Care, Toiletries			
Nails, Massage			
ENTERTAINMENT			
Movies, Videos			
CDs, Books			
Hobbies, Sports, Gym			
HEALTH CARE			
Prescriptions, Supplements			
Doctors, Dentists			
CHILDREN			
Child Care, Sitter			
Allowance, School Expense			
PETS			
Food, Supplies, Grooming			
MISCELLANEOUS			
Copies, Office Supplies			
Gifts, Cards			
Lottery			
Tithe, Donations			
TOTAL			
ATM WITHDRAWALS			
DEBIT CASH WITHDRAWALS			

THUR	FRI	SAT	SUN	TOTAL

NOVEMBER WEEK OF: _____

HOME	MON	TUES	WED
Groceries			
Meals Out			
Snacks, Beverages, Liquor			
Supplies, Furnishings			
TRANSPORTATION			
Gas, Public Transportation			
Vehicle Expense			
PERSONAL CARE			
Clothing, Accessories			
Laundry, Shoe Care			
Hair Care, Toiletries			
Nails, Massage			
ENTERTAINMENT			
Movies, Videos			
CDs, Books			
Hobbies, Sports, Gym			
HEALTH CARE			
Prescriptions, Supplements			
Doctors, Dentists			
CHILDREN			
Child Care, Sitter			
Allowance, School Expense			
PETS			
Food, Supplies, Grooming			
MISCELLANEOUS			
Copies, Office Supplies			
Gifts, Cards			
Lottery			
Tithe, Donations			
TOTAL			
ATM WITHDRAWALS			
DEBIT CASH WITHDRAWALS			

THUR	FRI	SAT	SUN	TOTAL

NOVEMBER WEEK OF: _____

HOME	MON	TUES	WED
Groceries			
Meals Out			
Snacks, Beverages, Liquor			
Supplies, Furnishings			
TRANSPORTATION			
Gas, Public Transportation			
Vehicle Expense			
PERSONAL CARE			
Clothing, Accessories			
Laundry, Shoe Care			
Hair Care, Toiletries			
Nails, Massage			
ENTERTAINMENT			
Movies, Videos			
CDs, Books			
Hobbies, Sports, Gym			
HEALTH CARE			
Prescriptions, Supplements			
Doctors, Dentists			
CHILDREN			
Child Care, Sitter			
Allowance, School Expense			
PETS			
Food, Supplies, Grooming			
MISCELLANEOUS			
Copies, Office Supplies			
Gifts, Cards			
Lottery			
Tithe, Donations			
TOTAL			
ATM WITHDRAWALS			
DEBIT CASH WITHDRAWALS			

THUR	FRI	SAT	SUN	TOTAL

NOVEMBER WEEK OF: _____

HOME	MON	TUES	WED
Groceries			
Meals Out			
Snacks, Beverages, Liquor			
Supplies, Furnishings			
TRANSPORTATION			
Gas, Public Transportation			
Vehicle Expense			
PERSONAL CARE			
Clothing, Accessories			
Laundry, Shoe Care			
Hair Care, Toiletries			
Nails, Massage			
ENTERTAINMENT			
Movies, Videos			
CDs, Books			
Hobbies, Sports, Gym			
HEALTH CARE			
Prescriptions, Supplements			
Doctors, Dentists			
CHILDREN			
Child Care, Sitter			
Allowance, School Expense			
PETS			
Food, Supplies, Grooming			
MISCELLANEOUS			
Copies, Office Supplies			
Gifts, Cards			
Lottery			
Tithe, Donations			
TOTAL			
ATM WITHDRAWALS			
DEBIT CASH WITHDRAWALS			

THUR	FRI	SAT	SUN	TOTAL

MONTHLY MONEY JOURNAL

(Notes/Reflections/Insights/Progress)

Use these pages to jot down your thoughts and experiences with money as you go through the month.

Did you notice any spending patterns?

....

....

....

Are there consistent thoughts or feelings you noticed when spending at certain times or on specific items?

....

....

....

Were you surprised at how much you spent in certain areas?

....

....

....

Were you delighted to see how long your money lasted or how little you spent in some areas?

....

....

....

Have you come up with changes you want to make?

....

....

....

Other comments:

....

....

....

....

SPLURGE DIARY

Use these pages for those times when your spending is totally unplanned and way over budget. By recording your feelings and circumstances about a particular spending event you can begin to get in touch with some deeper reasons for spending.

Date	What I bought or spent money on	Amount	Cash	Charge
....	....	....	....	....
....	....	....	....	....
....	....	....	....	....
....	....	....	....	....

What happened right before the spending?

....

....

....

How was I feeling at that time?

....

....

....

How did I feel during the spending?

....

....

....

How did I feel a few hours later?

....

....

....

Sample feelings: *depressed, angry, excited, empty, lonely, guilty, shamed, remorseful, anxious, frantic, bored, nervous, powerful, deserving, noticed, confused, worried, fearful, hopeless, accepted, resentful, overwhelmed, tired, needy, disappointed*

How did I feel the next day and/or a week later?

....

....

....

What did I do as a result of that spending?

....

....

....

What did I learn about myself (my habits, feelings, patterns, thoughts)?

....

....

....

What unmet needs am I possibly trying to meet through my spending?

....

....

....

Who or what do these feelings remind me of from my past?

....

....

....

Next time, what can I do to replace the spending urge?
(See Alternative Activities List.)

....

....

....

Changes I've made since that spending:

....

....

....

Notes/Reflections/Insights:

VICTORY DIARY

Use these pages for those times when you *successfully did not give in* to your spending urges. Changing your spending patterns is a very positive and significant event, so acknowledge yourself on these occasions.

Date	What I *almost* bought or spent money on	Amount	Cash	Charge
....	....	....	....	....
....	....	....	....	....
....	....	....	....	....
....	....	....	....	....

What happened right before the spending urge?

....

....

....

How was I feeling at that time?

....

....

....

What did I do to *replace* the spending urge?

....

....

....

How did I feel immediately after deciding *not* to spend the money?

....

....

....

Sample feelings: *powerful, in charge, victorious, calm, relaxed, happy, proud, content, honest, satisfied, hopeful, validated, accepted, delighted, responsible, free*

How did I feel a few hours later?

....

....

....

How did I feel the next day and/or a week later?

....

....

....

What did I learn about myself (my habits, feelings, patterns, beliefs)?

....

....

....

I am proud of myself because:

....

....

....

How did I reward myself (praised myself, read a book, prepared a pleasant meal, took a nap, spent time on crafts or hobbies, took a drive, walked the dog, etc.)?

....

....

....

Notes/Reflections/Insights:

ALTERNATIVE ACTIVITIES LIST

For Replacing Spending Urges

Having the urge to spend, for some people, can be a very powerful feeling, so it is not easy to just *will it away*. When the urge comes up, you might try postponing it by engaging in another activity. I have listed some low-cost, no-cost activity ideas to help you gradually find ways to replace those urges with new, more positive behavior.

Try them out and see what works best for you. Your ideas are probably the most creative, so be sure to add many of your own.

These suggestions are especially effective if you are at the stage where you recognize you have behaviors and feelings associated with spending money. If your spending behavior has become much more serious and feels out of control, please see the Resource Guide in the back of the book for help.

Instead of spending at this particular time, I can . . .

✔ *Use the 24-hour technique: Tell yourself that you can buy this item. You can buy it tomorrow. You are choosing to wait 24 hours.*

- ✔ *Call a supportive friend or sponsor and talk about the events of the day and your feelings*

- ✔ *Take a walk or a drive, bike ride, hike, rollerblade or go to the gym*

- ✔ *Read a good story in a book or magazine*

- ✔ *Spend time on your favorite hobby or craft*

- ✔ *Watch a great movie*

- ✔ *Take in a museum, zoo or the botanical gardens*

- ✔ *Play with your children or your pets*

- ✔ *Have your partner give you a massage*

- ✔ *Take a bath or a nap*

- ✔ *Listen to music*

- ✔ *Meditate*

- ✔ *Now add your own*

My favorite activities to do or new things to try are:

....

....

....

....

....

DECEMBER

Questions to ponder when reviewing
finances or right before spending . . .

**What would happen if I did not spend as much
money on gifts for everyone this year?**

**Do I tend to always buy the biggest, the best
and with the most "bells and whistles"?**

**As I review my spending this year, am I beginning
to feel like I might finally have a sense of
enough of something?**

---

*"There are no unrealistic goals, only unrealistic time
frames."*

Carol Park, Founder, MoneyLife
Cupertino, Calif.

My Success Story

My financial situation before I started this book was:

....

....

After recording my expenses, I noticed:

....

....

I made the following changes in my spending and/or thinking:

....

....

From these changes, I gained or learned:

....

....

My goals for next year are:

....

....

DECEMBER WEEK OF: _____

HOME	MON	TUES	WED
Groceries			
Meals Out			
Snacks, Beverages, Liquor			
Supplies, Furnishings			
TRANSPORTATION			
Gas, Public Transportation			
Vehicle Expense			
PERSONAL CARE			
Clothing, Accessories			
Laundry, Shoe Care			
Hair Care, Toiletries			
Nails, Massage			
ENTERTAINMENT			
Movies, Videos			
CDs, Books			
Hobbies, Sports, Gym			
HEALTH CARE			
Prescriptions, Supplements			
Doctors, Dentists			
CHILDREN			
Child Care, Sitter			
Allowance, School Expense			
PETS			
Food, Supplies, Grooming			
MISCELLANEOUS			
Copies, Office Supplies			
Gifts, Cards			
Lottery			
Tithe, Donations			
TOTAL			
ATM WITHDRAWALS			
DEBIT CASH WITHDRAWALS			

THUR	FRI	SAT	SUN	TOTAL

DECEMBER   WEEK OF: _____

HOME	MON	TUES	WED
Groceries			
Meals Out			
Snacks, Beverages, Liquor			
Supplies, Furnishings			
TRANSPORTATION			
Gas, Public Transportation			
Vehicle Expense			
PERSONAL CARE			
Clothing, Accessories			
Laundry, Shoe Care			
Hair Care, Toiletries			
Nails, Massage			
ENTERTAINMENT			
Movies, Videos			
CDs, Books			
Hobbies, Sports, Gym			
HEALTH CARE			
Prescriptions, Supplements			
Doctors, Dentists			
CHILDREN			
Child Care, Sitter			
Allowance, School Expense			
PETS			
Food, Supplies, Grooming			
MISCELLANEOUS			
Copies, Office Supplies			
Gifts, Cards			
Lottery			
Tithe, Donations			
TOTAL			
ATM WITHDRAWALS			
DEBIT CASH WITHDRAWALS			

THUR	FRI	SAT	SUN	TOTAL

DECEMBER WEEK OF: _____

HOME	MON	TUES	WED
Groceries			
Meals Out			
Snacks, Beverages, Liquor			
Supplies, Furnishings			
TRANSPORTATION			
Gas, Public Transportation			
Vehicle Expense			
PERSONAL CARE			
Clothing, Accessories			
Laundry, Shoe Care			
Hair Care, Toiletries			
Nails, Massage			
ENTERTAINMENT			
Movies, Videos			
CDs, Books			
Hobbies, Sports, Gym			
HEALTH CARE			
Prescriptions, Supplements			
Doctors, Dentists			
CHILDREN			
Child Care, Sitter			
Allowance, School Expense			
PETS			
Food, Supplies, Grooming			
MISCELLANEOUS			
Copies, Office Supplies			
Gifts, Cards			
Lottery			
Tithe, Donations			
TOTAL			
ATM WITHDRAWALS			
DEBIT CASH WITHDRAWALS			

THUR	FRI	SAT	SUN	TOTAL

DECEMBER WEEK OF: _____

HOME	MON	TUES	WED
Groceries			
Meals Out			
Snacks, Beverages, Liquor			
Supplies, Furnishings			
TRANSPORTATION			
Gas, Public Transportation			
Vehicle Expense			
PERSONAL CARE			
Clothing, Accessories			
Laundry, Shoe Care			
Hair Care, Toiletries			
Nails, Massage			
ENTERTAINMENT			
Movies, Videos			
CDs, Books			
Hobbies, Sports, Gym			
HEALTH CARE			
Prescriptions, Supplements			
Doctors, Dentists			
CHILDREN			
Child Care, Sitter			
Allowance, School Expense			
PETS			
Food, Supplies, Grooming			
MISCELLANEOUS			
Copies, Office Supplies			
Gifts, Cards			
Lottery			
Tithe, Donations			
TOTAL			
ATM WITHDRAWALS			
DEBIT CASH WITHDRAWALS			

THUR	FRI	SAT	SUN	TOTAL

DECEMBER WEEK OF: _____

HOME	MON	TUES	WED
Groceries			
Meals Out			
Snacks, Beverages, Liquor			
Supplies, Furnishings			
TRANSPORTATION			
Gas, Public Transportation			
Vehicle Expense			
PERSONAL CARE			
Clothing, Accessories			
Laundry, Shoe Care			
Hair Care, Toiletries			
Nails, Massage			
ENTERTAINMENT			
Movies, Videos			
CDs, Books			
Hobbies, Sports, Gym			
HEALTH CARE			
Prescriptions, Supplements			
Doctors, Dentists			
CHILDREN			
Child Care, Sitter			
Allowance, School Expense			
PETS			
Food, Supplies, Grooming			
MISCELLANEOUS			
Copies, Office Supplies			
Gifts, Cards			
Lottery			
Tithe, Donations			
TOTAL			
ATM WITHDRAWALS			
DEBIT CASH WITHDRAWALS			

THUR	FRI	SAT	SUN	TOTAL

MONTHLY MONEY JOURNAL

(Notes/Reflections/Insights/Progress)

Use these pages to jot down your thoughts and experiences with money as you go through the month.

Did you notice any spending patterns?

....

....

....

Are there consistent thoughts or feelings you noticed when spending at certain times or on specific items?

....

....

....

Were you surprised at how much you spent in certain areas?

....

....

....

Were you delighted to see how long your money lasted or how little you spent in some areas?

....

....

....

Have you come up with changes you want to make?

....

....

....

Other comments:

....

....

....

....

SPLURGE DIARY

Use these pages for those times when your spending is totally unplanned and way over budget. By recording your feelings and circumstances about a particular spending event you can begin to get in touch with some deeper reasons for spending.

Date	What I bought or spent money on	Amount	Cash	Charge
....	....	....	....	....
....	....	....	....	....
....	....	....	....	....
....	....	....	....	....

What happened right before the spending?

....

....

....

How was I feeling at that time?

....

....

....

How did I feel during the spending?

....

....

....

How did I feel a few hours later?

....

....

....

Sample feelings: *depressed, angry, excited, empty, lonely, guilty, shamed, remorseful, anxious, frantic, bored, nervous, powerful, deserving, noticed, confused, worried, fearful, hopeless, accepted, resentful, overwhelmed, tired, needy, disappointed*

How did I feel the next day and/or a week later?

....

....

....

What did I do as a result of that spending?

....

....

....

What did I learn about myself (my habits, feelings, patterns, thoughts)?

....

....

....

What unmet needs am I possibly trying to meet through my spending?

....

....

....

Who or what do these feelings remind me of from my past?

....

....

....

Next time, what can I do to replace the spending urge?
(See Alternative Activities List.)

....

....

....

Changes I've made since that spending:

....

....

....

Notes/Reflections/Insights:

VICTORY DIARY

Use these pages for those times when you *successfully did not give in* to your spending urges. Changing your spending patterns is a very positive and significant event, so acknowledge yourself on these occasions.

Date	What I *almost* bought or spent money on	Amount	Cash	Charge
....	....	....	....	....
....	....	....	....	....
....	....	....	....	....
....	....	....	....	....

What happened right before the spending urge?

....

....

....

How was I feeling at that time?

....

....

....

What did I do to *replace* the spending urge?

....

....

....

How did I feel immediately after deciding *not* to spend the money?

....

....

....

Sample feelings: *powerful, in charge, victorious, calm, relaxed, happy, proud, content, honest, satisfied, hopeful, validated, accepted, delighted, responsible, free*

How did I feel a few hours later?

....

....

....

How did I feel the next day and/or a week later?

....

....

....

What did I learn about myself (my habits, feelings, patterns, beliefs)?

....

....

....

I am proud of myself because:

....

....

....

How did I reward myself (praised myself, read a book, prepared a pleasant meal, took a nap, spent time on crafts or hobbies, took a drive, walked the dog, etc.)?

....

....

....

Notes/Reflections/Insights:

ALTERNATIVE ACTIVITIES LIST

For Replacing Spending Urges

Having the urge to spend, for some people, can be a very powerful feeling, so it is not easy to just *will it away*. When the urge comes up, you might try postponing it by engaging in another activity. I have listed some low-cost, no-cost activity ideas to help you gradually find ways to replace those urges with new, more positive behavior.

Try them out and see what works best for you. Your ideas are probably the most creative, so be sure to add many of your own.

These suggestions are especially effective if you are at the stage where you recognize you have behaviors and feelings associated with spending money. If your spending behavior has become much more serious and feels out of control, please see the Resource Guide in the back of the book for help.

Instead of spending at this particular time, I can . . .

✔ *Use the 24-hour technique: Tell yourself that you can buy this item. You can buy it tomorrow. You are choosing to wait 24 hours.*

- ✔ *Call a supportive friend or sponsor and talk about the events of the day and your feelings*

- ✔ *Take a walk or a drive, bike ride, hike, rollerblade or go to the gym*

- ✔ *Read a good story in a book or magazine*

- ✔ *Spend time on your favorite hobby or craft*

- ✔ *Watch a great movie*

- ✔ *Take in a museum, zoo or the botanical gardens*

- ✔ *Play with your children or your pets*

- ✔ *Have your partner give you a massage*

- ✔ *Take a bath or a nap*

- ✔ *Listen to music*

- ✔ *Meditate*

- ✔ *Now add your own*

My favorite activities to do or new things to try are:

....

....

....

....

....

MONEY TRACKER YEARLY SUMMARY

HOME	JAN	FEB
Groceries		
Meals Out		
Snacks, Beverages, Liquor		
Supplies, Furnishings		
TRANSPORTATION		
Gas, Public Transportation		
Vehicle Expense		
PERSONAL CARE		
Clothing, Accessories		
Laundry, Shoe Care		
Hair Care, Toiletries		
Nails, Massage		
ENTERTAINMENT		
Movies, Videos		
CDs, Books		
Hobbies, Sports, Gym		
HEALTH CARE		
Prescriptions, Supplements		
Doctors, Dentists		
CHILDREN		
Child Care, Sitter		
Allowance, School Expense		
PETS		
Food, Supplies, Grooming		
MISCELLANEOUS		
Copies, Office Supplies		
Gifts, Cards		
Lottery		
Tithe, Donations		
TOTAL		
ATM WITHDRAWALS		
DEBIT CASH WITHDRAWALS		

MAR	APR	MAY	JUNE

MONEY TRACKER YEARLY SUMMARY

HOME	JULY	AUG
Groceries		
Meals Out		
Snacks, Beverages, Liquor		
Supplies, Furnishings		
TRANSPORTATION		
Gas, Public Transportation		
Vehicle Expense		
PERSONAL CARE		
Clothing, Accessories		
Laundry, Shoe Care		
Hair Care, Toiletries		
Nails, Massage		
ENTERTAINMENT		
Movies, Videos		
CDs, Books		
Hobbies, Sports, Gym		
HEALTH CARE		
Prescriptions, Supplements		
Doctors, Dentists		
CHILDREN		
Child Care, Sitter		
Allowance, School Expense		
PETS		
Food, Supplies, Grooming		
MISCELLANEOUS		
Copies, Office Supplies		
Gifts, Cards		
Lottery		
Tithe, Donations		
TOTAL		
ATM WITHDRAWALS		
DEBIT CASH WITHDRAWALS		

SEPT	OCT	NOV	DEC	TOTAL

RESOURCE GUIDE

The following resources can offer basic financial skills, support groups and psychological guidance depending upon your needs. The list of book titles will also give you a sampling of the numerous books available at bookstores and libraries.

General Financial Help Resources

Consumer Credit Counseling Service (CCCS)
For referrals to your local nonprofit agency,
phone 1-800-388-2227
These nonprofit agencies provide free or low-cost education and counseling programs on personal budgeting issues and debt-reduction programs.

National Foundation for Consumer Credit
8611 Second Avenue, Suite 100
Silver Spring, MD 20910
301-589-5600

BHA Bankcard Consumer News Newsletter
Bankcard Holders of America
524 Branch Drive
Salem, VA 24153
540-389-5445
A nonprofit consumer organization dedicated to helping bankcard holders become informed consumers

Telephone Counseling
Judy Lawrence
505-296-8792
I offer financial counseling by telephone on an hourly fee basis.

Money-Saving Newsletters

To review a copy of these newsletters, send a self-addressed stamped envelope with $1 to the address listed:

Penny Pincher
P.O. Box 809
Kings Park, NY 11754-0809

The Pocket Change Investor, Good Advice Press
Box 78
Elizaville, NY 12523

Skinflint News
1460 Noell Blvd.
Palm Harbor, FL 34683-5639

Tightwad Gazette
R.R.1, Box 3570
Leeds, ME 04263

There is also an excellent selection of books at your local library or bookstore providing frugal lifestyle ideas and money-saving tips.

Books—Basic Money Management

The Budget Kit: The Common Cent$ Money Management Workbook, by Judy Lawrence (Dearborn Financial Publishing, 1993)

The Guide to Personal Budgeting: How to Stretch Your Dollars Through Wise Money Management, by David Scott (Globe Pequot Press, 1995)

How To Get What You Want in Life with the Money You Already Have, by Carol Keeffe (Little, Brown and Company, 1995)

The Money Diet: Reaping the Rewards of Financial Fitness, by Ginger Applegarth, CFP, CLU, AhFC (Penguin, 1995)

Ninety Days to Financial Fitness, by Joan German-Grapes (Collier Books, 1993)

Personal Finance for Dummies, by Eric Tyson (IDG Books, 1995)

Richest Man in Babylon, by George S. Clason (Signet, 1955)

The Way To Save: A 10-Step Blueprint for Lifetime Security, by Ginita Wall, CPA (Henry Holt & Co., 1993)

Your Personal Financial Fitness Program: A Step by Step Guide to Managing Your Money, by Elizabeth S. Lewin, CFP (Facts on File, 1995)

Personal Self-Help Resources

To get a listing of your local Debtor's Anonymous meetings, call or write for information:

Debtor's Anonymous General Service Office
P.O. Box 400
Grand Central Station
New York, NY 10163-0400
212-642-8220

Debtor's Anonymous meeting hotline for New York and the Tri-State Area: 212-969-8111

Addiction Therapists or Treatment Centers
When seeking help in your local area, ask for a certified addictions counselor.

National Self Help Clearinghouse
25 West 43rd St., Suite 620
New York, NY 10036
212-354-8525
Call or send a self-addressed stamped envelope for a referral to a regional self-help clearinghouse in your area to find information on 12-step groups, Gambler's Anonymous and non-12-step groups to give support with personal issues.

Books—Money and Addictions (Recovery/Self-Help)

Born to Spend: How to Overcome Compulsive Spending, by Gloria Arenson (TAB Books, 1992)

Can't Buy Me Love: Freedom from Compulsive Spending and Money Obsession, by Sally Coleman, MA, and Nancy Hull-Mast (Fairview Press, Minneapolis, 1992)

Credit Cash and Co-Dependency, by Yvonne Kaye, PhD (Health Communications, Inc., 1991)

Financial Recovery Workbook: A Practical Guide to Creating Your Spending Plan, Reducing Your Debt, Understanding Your Money Behavior, by Karen McCall (Financial Recovery, San Anselmo, Calif., 1995)

How to Get Out of Debt, Stay Out of Debt & Live Prosperously (Based on the Proven Principles and Techniques of Debtors Anonymous), by Jerrold Mundis (Bantam Books, 1988)

Money Demons: Keep Them from Sabotaging Your Relationships—and Your Life, by Susan Forward (Bantam Books, 1994)

Money Harmony: Resolving Money Conflicts in Your Life and Relationships, by Olivia Mellan (Walker and Company, 1995)

The Money Drunk: 90 Days to Financial Sobriety, by Mark Bryan and Julia Cameron (Ballantine, 1993)

Overcoming Overspending: A Winning Plan for Spenders and Their Partners, by Olivia Mellan (Walker and Company, 1995)

Shopaholics: Serious Help for Addicted Spenders, by Janet E. Damon (Price Stern Sloan, 1988) (This book may be out of print, but well worth looking for at your local library or used bookstore.)

EXPENSE SUPPLEMENT

Many of the categories are self-explanatory. Below are specific expense suggestions to include in each category and to help you remember your own specific spending.

Home

Groceries	In addition to supermarkets, remember groceries from: Health food stores, Warehouses, Convenience stores (gas stations), Delis, Farmer's market
Meals Out	In addition to sit-down meals in restaurants, remember to record: Fast-food, Take-out food, Concession stand meals
Snacks, Beverages, Liquor	Coffee, Tea, Soft drinks (whether from vending machine, fast-food stop or convenience store), Bottled water, Bagels, Muffins, Cookies, Candy, Chips, Popcorn, Yogurt, Ice cream, Beer, Wine, Drinks

Supplies, **Furnishings**	Cleaning supplies, Organizers, Linens, Housewares, Plants, Bedded flowers, Herbs, Yard and lawn supplies, Cut or dry flowers, Wall hangings, Candles, Vases, Knickknacks, Baskets, Crafts, Holiday items

Transportation

Gas, Public ***Transportation***	Bus, Train, Subway, Taxi, Carpool
Vehicle Expense	Parking, Tolls, Car wash, Lube job, Maintenance, Misc. supplies

Personal Care

Clothing, ***Accessories***	Business, Formal, Casual, Sport, Gym, Shoes, Coats, Undergarments, Belts, Caps, Hats, Scarves, Jewelry, Hair accessories, Children's clothing (here or under Children below)
Laundry, ***Shoe Care***	Dry cleaning, Laundromat, Alterations, Tailoring, Shoe repair, Shoe shine
Hair Care, ***Toiletries***	Beauty salon, Barber, Haircut, Color, Perm, Hair care products, Cosmetics, Oils, Lotions, Soaps, Personal
Nails, Massage	Manicure, Pedicure, Rebase, Massage, Herbal wraps, Facial, Other body work, Hair removal and other personal care

Entertainment

Movies, Videos

Popcorn, Drink & snacks (here or under Food above), Video rentals, Late fees, Family activities (Water Park, Golf, Children's play centers), Sports events, Concerts, Theater

CDs, Books

Cassette tapes, Albums, Newspapers, Magazines, Software, Electronic supplies

Hobbies, Sports, Gym

Lessons, Hobby, Craft supplies & fees, Sports equipment, Supplies & entrance fees, Gym fees & supplies

Health Care

Copayments (Include these expenses if you pay a copay on-site.)

Prescriptions, Supplements

Drugs, Medical supplies, Glasses, Frames, Contacts & supplies, Herbs, Vitamins & minerals, Homeopathic remedies, Health store misc. supplies

Doctors, Dentists

Specialists, Eye exams, Lab work, Chiropractor, Acupuncturist, Nutritionist, Physical therapist, Therapist, Counselor

Children

Child Care, Sitter

Baby-sitters, Gym day care

| *Allowance, School Expense* | College money, "Gimme money," School lunch, Supplies, Field trips, Fund raisers, School events, Sports, Equipment, Fees, Magazines, Books, CDs, Tapes, Software, Games, Lessons (Music, Dance, Costumes), Hobbies, Crafts, Arcades, Toys, Diapers |

Pets

| *Food, Supplies, Grooming* | Diet food, Treats, Toys, Shots, Medications, Vet visits, Boarding, Nail cutting, Teeth cleaning, Other |

Miscellaneous

Copies, Office Supplies	Faxes, Postage, Shipping expense, Organizers, Software
Gifts, Cards	Birthday, Anniversary, Mother's & Father's Day, Religious events, Weddings, Baby showers, Flowers, Favors, Host gift
Lottery	Bingo, Gambling
Tithe, Donations, Spiritual Items	Charitable giving, Countertop donations, Support meetings, Sunday donation, Rosaries, Candles, Chimes
Other	Cigarettes, Pipes, Cigars, Tobacco, Film & developing, Pay phone, Tips

3 Easy Ways to Order

1. By Mail:
Mail to:
Dearborn Multimedia
155 N. Wacker Drive
Chicago, IL 60606

2. By FAX:
FAX your order
(with credit card information)
to: 1-312-836-9958

3. By Phone:
Call Toll-Free
(credit card orders only)
1-800-638-0375
Have your Visa, MasterCard,
or American Express handy.

Name_____

Address_____

City_____

State_____ Zip_____

Phone (   )_____

❑ Personal Check Enclosed (checks payable to: Dearborn Financial Publishing)

Credit Card Information   ❑ Visa   ❑ MasterCard   ❑ AMEX

Account #_____ Exp. Date_____

Signature_____

Order No.	Title	Price	Qty.	Total

Subtotal	
Sales Tax (CA, FL, IL and NY only)	
Shipping & Handling $5.00	
Total	

Dearborn Multimedia
155 North Wacker Drive
Chicago, IL 60606
1-800-638-0375

Source Code 605114